Royal Geographical Society Exploring Series

EXPLORING ANTARCTICA

Ian Cameron

Longman

Contents

Royal Geographical Society

Exploring Antarctica has been written with the help of the Royal Geographical Society. This Society has been working for more than 150 years *"for the promotion of that most important and entertaining branch of knowledge, geography."* In the past it sponsored many of the world's great explorers – Livingstone in Africa, Scott and Shackleton in the Antarctic, Hillary and Tenzing on Everest. Today it is busier than ever. It has the world's largest private collection of maps, and a magnificent library; its publications and lectures play a leading role in geographical teaching and research; more than 100 expeditions apply to it annually for help, and each year it sends large numbers of explorers, research-workers, scientists and conservationists to the farthest ends of the Earth.

I should like to thank the Royal Geographical Society very much indeed for their support and encouragement, for allowing me the use of their library, map-room and archives, and for providing most of the book's illustrations.

Ian Cameron

Cover: Travelling by sledge in Antarctica.

Back cover: Endurance *trapped in the pack ice.*

Endpapers: Ice floe and icebergs, Bellingshausen Sea.

Title page: Dumont D'Urville's ships Astrolabe *and* Zelée *fighting for their lives in the pack ice.*

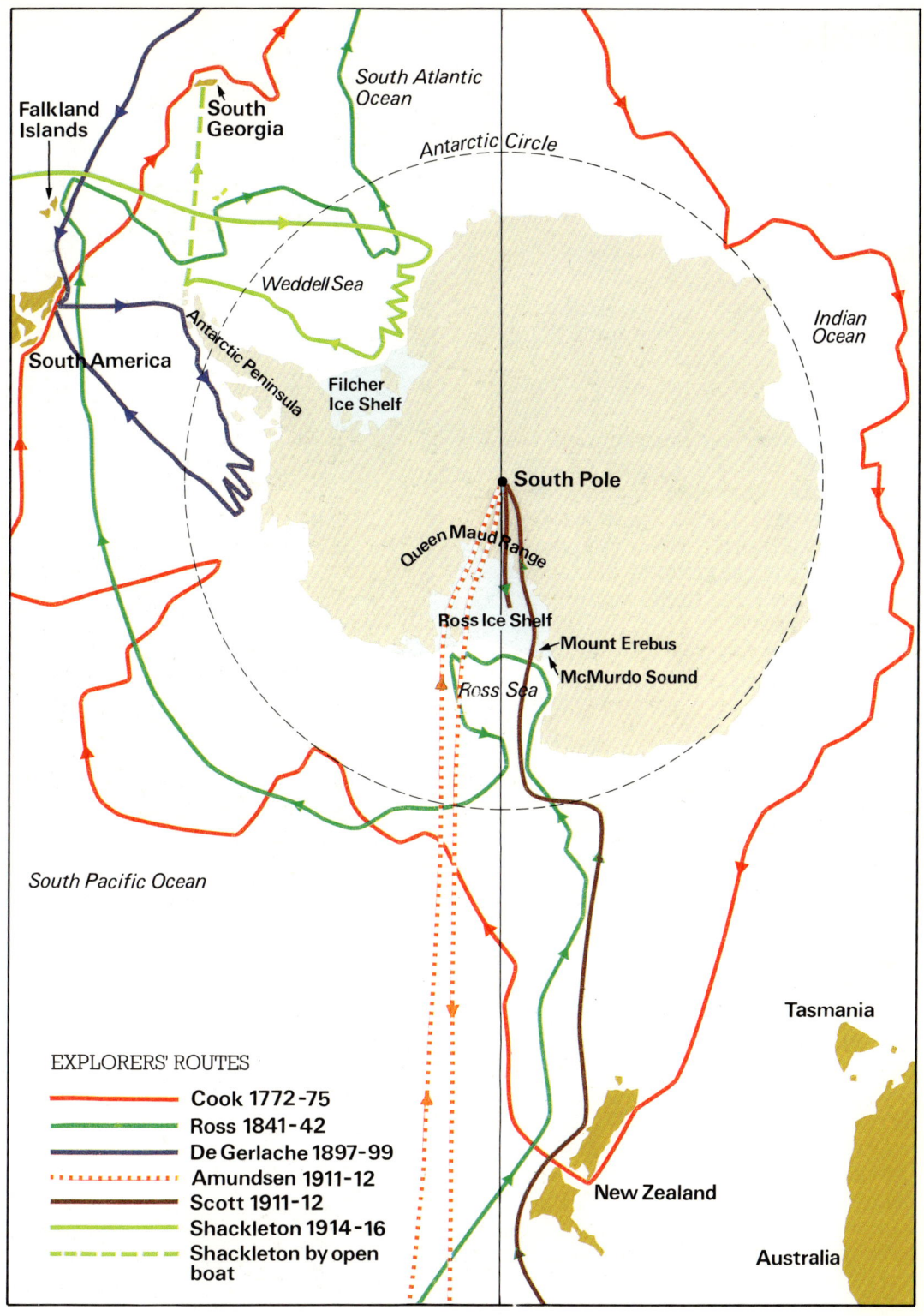

Falkland
Islands

South
Georgia

*South Atlantic
Ocean*

Antarctic Circle

Weddell Sea

*Indian
Ocean*

South America

Antarctic Peninsula

Filcher
Ice Shelf

● **South Pole**

Queen Maud Range

Ross Ice Shelf

← Mount Erebus

← McMurdo Sound

Ross Sea

South Pacific Ocean

Tasmania

New Zealand

Australia

EXPLORERS' ROUTES

————	Cook 1772-75
————	Ross 1841-42
————	De Gerlache 1897-99
··········	Amundsen 1911-12
————	Scott 1911-12
————	Shackleton 1914-16
– – – –	Shackleton by open boat

Antarctica: A World of Ice

Area: 14,000,000 square kilometres
Mean elevation: 1,800 metres
Highest point: Mount Markham (4,600 metres)
Highest recorded temperature: 13.9°C (Hope Bay, Antarctic Peninsula)
Lowest recorded temperature: −88°C (Vostok)

The name Antarctica comes from two Greek words, *anti* meaning opposite, and *arctos* meaning bear. The cluster of stars above the North Pole was called *arctos* by the Greeks because of its bearlike shape. Over the years *arctos*, corrupted to arctic, became accepted as the name, not only for the stars, but for the North Polar regions on which they shine. The South Polar regions, on the opposite side of the world, became known as the *anti* (or opposite) arctic. This in time was shortened to Antarctic.

*   *   *

Astronauts tell us that when they see our planet from space its most impressive feature is Antarctica, which *"radiates light like a great beacon across the bottom of the world."* Antarctica radiates light because it is covered by an enormous ice-cap. This ice-cap extends over 14 million square kilometres (an area far larger than the U.S.A.). Its *average* thickness is over 2,000 metres. It contains more than 90% of the world's ice and snow. If the ice and snow suddenly melted the oceans would rise to such a height that half the people on Earth would be drowned.

The story of how this great ice-continent was discovered and explored is a story of hazardous voyages, epic treks, and, above all, human endurance. Nowhere else on Earth have explorers had to face so many difficulties and dangers.

The first of these difficulties is that Antarctica

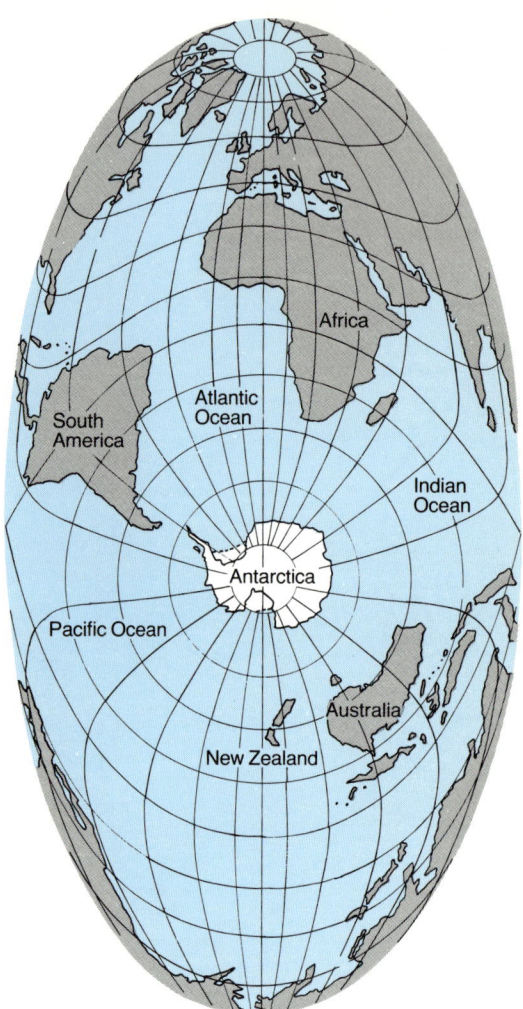

The Earth as a flat ellipse, showing Antarctica in relation to the other continents.

is so remote. If you look at the map above you will see that whereas the Arctic is an ocean surrounded by the populated landmasses of Europe, America and Asia, the Antarctic is a continent, set in splendid isolation and divided from the rest of the world by vast reaches of sea. Today, thanks to air travel, this remoteness is not a major problem. However, in the 18th and early 19th centuries the greater part of the southern hemisphere was unknown. Ports like Buenos Aires, Sydney and Wellington didn't exist. The early explorers had therefore to travel something like 16,000 kilometres before they could even begin to explore.

When they did at last approach Antarctica,

Entrance to Lemaire Channel, Antarctic Peninsula.

they found that the continent, like a medieval fortress, has outer bastions of defence.

The first of these barriers is the Southern Ocean, where explorers found the most tempestuous seas on Earth. The Southern Ocean lies between the 50th and 70th latitudes. A glance at the map will confirm that in these latitudes there is no land apart from the tip of Tierra del Fuego and a scattering of bleak little islands. Winds and waves are therefore able to build up into a continuous storm-belt which blows non-stop around the Earth. Here the *average* windspeed is only a little less than 65 km/h, which means that night and day there is more or less constant Force 8 gale, with gusts of hurricane velocity recorded many times a month. Even on relatively calm days there is a 5-metre swell in the Southern Ocean; while in days of storm great waves, a kilometre from crest to crest and 18 metres from trough to summit, roll endlessly out of the west like wave after wave of charging cavalry, their spear-tips great sheets of horizontal spume. Modern freighters have been known to founder under their bludgeoning.

Those who manage to force their way through these dangerous waters, are then brought up short by the continent's second line of defence: pack-ice.

Antarctica is ringed by a continuous girdle of sea-ice, which may be anything from one centimetre to six metres in thickness, and anything from fifteen kilometres to fifteen hundred kilometres in width. This pack-ice is never still. It drifts this way and that under the influence of currents and winds, expanding and contracting according to temperature and season. In summer its area may be less than that of Europe, in winter it may be greater than that of the United States and Canada combined. For ten months out of twelve it is impenetrable. It is not a good place in which to be caught by bad weather. *"Our ships,"* wrote James Clark Ross, the first explorer to force his way through it,

9

Penguins, painted by Edward Wilson.

have to face the most formidable of Antarctica's defences: the weather, and in particular the cold and the wind.

Antarctica is by far the coldest place on Earth. Its weather stations often report temperatures of below −80°C, more than 20° lower than anywhere else. *"In this sort of cold,"* writes the explorer John Berchervaise, *"if you drop a steel bar it is likely to shatter like glass, tin disintegrates into loose granules, mercury freezes into a solid metal, and if you haul up a fish through a hole in the ice within five seconds it is frozen so solid it has to be cut with a saw."* Another explorer, Douglas Mawson, describes the wind as Antarctica's "most malevolent characteristic". When he wintered in Adélie Land gusts of over 240 km/h were frequently recorded and the *average* windspeed for June was 101·9 km/h. *"In these conditions"* (he writes) *"it was possible to stand for no more than a few seconds, and then only by leaning forward at an angle of 45°!"*

If you compare the Arctic to the Antarctic, the former is a positive hothouse! North of the Arctic Circle tens of thousands of families live in comfort all the year round. Thousands of plants and animals, including human beings, are able to survive; hundreds of children are born every year. But south of the Antarctic Circle there is no habitation that people can call their home. The only plants are a handful of mosses and lichens. The only landlife are one-celled protozea and wingless flies. Until recently no human child had ever been born. (In the last few years a number of Argentine mothers have given birth to their children in Antarctica, in order to try to establish Argentina's territorial claims.)

Two hundred years ago no-one had ever set eyes on this desolate but bleakly beautiful continent. Since the dawn of time it had lain hidden behind tempestuous seas and near-impenetrable ice, marked on the maps only as *Terra Australis nondum cognita*, the Unknown Southern Continent, which, it was believed, must exist to counterbalance the landmass of Eurasia.

The first person to discover what sort of place this southern continent really is was Captain Cook.

"rolled and groaned amidst the blocks of ice over which the ocean rolled its mountainous waves, throwing huge masses one upon another then burying them deep beneath its foaming waters, the while dashing and grinding them together with fearful violence. The awful grandeur of such a scene can neither be imagined nor described."

Only when the Southern Ocean has been crossed and the pack-ice breached can explorers land on the continent itself. They then

1 The Myth of the Great Southern Continent

There was something unusual about the ships that lay anchored in Plymouth Sound, and about their commanding officer and their orders.

The ships, the *Resolution* and *Adventure*, flew the white ensign (the flag of the Royal Navy); yet they were not men-of-war. They were Whitby colliers: small trading vessels, with enormous holds to enable them to carry a profitable cargo, and a shallow draught to enable them to work close inshore. Their lines were more comfortable than elegant, and their hulls were encased not with the usual copper but with a double-sheathing of oak. They were not impressive-looking.

Their commanding officer was not impressive-looking either. Fashionable court painters like Nathaniel Dance depict Captain James Cook as a classically handsome man (the portrait on p.15). This is wrong. Good painters who knew him because they sailed with him, like William Hodges, depict him as small-boned and sharp-featured, with a shock of unruly hair (the portrait on p.12). He was one of the few senior naval officers of his generation to have worked his way up from the lower deck.

Cook's orders were to "discover and take possession of convenient stations in the Great South Land." This was a tough assignment. For although the Great South Land had appeared on maps for something like 2,000 years, no-one had ever set eyes on it.

The myth of a Great Southern Continent was started by the Greeks. It was Aristotle who first put forward the theory that the Earth was a sphere – because, he argued, no shape except a sphere could account for the ever-shifting horizon, and the disappearance as one travels north or south of familiar stars. And his school of philosophers took his logic a step further.

Knowing that the northern part of the Earth consisted of a huge landmass (Eurasia), they argued that in order to balance this the southern part of the Earth must consist of a similar landmass. It was 1,500 years before the Greeks were known to be right about their spherical Earth; then Magellan proved Aristotle's point by sailing round the world. It seemed to cartographers that since the Greeks had been right about their spherical Earth, they were probably right too about their Great Southern Continent. So for the next 250 years the most enormous "Land of Brazil Wood, Elephants and Gold" appeared on every map: a mythical continent, to balance Eurasia, filling the greater part of the southern hemisphere. When the seamen of a dozen nations went in search of this fabled South Land and failed to find it, one might have thought its existence would soon be doubted. On the contrary. Whenever an explorer discovered new lands in the southern hemisphere (the Solomon Islands in 1568, the Falkland Islands in 1592, Australia in 1616, and Kerguélen Island in 1772) cartographers inked-in the landfalls on their maps, and joined them together to form a continuous coastline! Dreams die hard. And to quote the historian H.R. Mill: *"right up to the middle of the 18th century the southern hemisphere figured on all maps as the seat of a great continent, awaiting discovery."*

It was to take possession of this unknown continent that Cook sailed from Plymouth on 13th July, 1772.

Before *Resolution* had cleared the English Channel, the crew discovered that their captain had revolutionary ideas about how a ship should be run. In particular he was determined they should never get scurvy.

This terrible disease often killed 60% or even 70% of a ship's company. It was caused partly by a lack of fresh vegetables (and hence vitamin C), and partly by the unbelievable squalour of life below-decks. Cook, once an able seaman, knew all about life below-decks. At the end of his first voyage his captain's report had read: *"Put ashore at the hospital 130 men, most of which are extremely ill: buried the last month 22."* Cook was determined that no ship under his command should ever be-

come such a charnel-house. So he filled *Resolution's* ample hold with vegetables: *"8,000 lbs* (3,630 kilograms) *of cabbage cut fine and cured in brine, 1,000 string of antiscorbutic onions, much mermerlade of oranges and lemons."* Cook also insisted on a standard of hygiene hitherto undreamed of. He allowed his crew to keep three watches instead of the usual two, thus ensuring they had plenty of sleep. He made every man, even in the Antarctic, have at least one cold bath a day. Hammocks, clothing and bedding were brought on deck every three days for airing. Once a week *Resolution* was either "cured with fires" or "smoked clean with a mixture of vinegar and gunpowder." Cook made frequent inspections of every part of his ship and every member of his crew. There was some discontent at first at so strict a routine. "Every day is Sunday (i.e. a captain's round's day) with Mr. Cook!" one of the crew complained. But events were to prove he was justified.

After a brief stay in Cape Town to take aboard fresh vegetables, Cook sailed south into unknown waters. For the first time in history Antarctica's defences were about to be tested by a well-found expedition led by a first-class seaman who was determined, in his own words, "to go as far as it is possible for man to go."

As *Resolution* and *Adventure* headed into the Indian Ocean, the weather was appalling: heavy seas, high winds and bitter cold. And soon, in much the same latitude as London in the northern hemisphere, Cook was brought up short by pack ice. This demonstrates the main difference between the northern and southern hemispheres. In the northern hemisphere, ice extends only some 1,500 kilometres from the Pole; in the southern hemisphere it extends for 5,000 kilometres. For several months Cook followed the edge of the pack-ice; always trying to force his way south, but always being thwarted by ice too thick to penetrate. His Diary for 15th December (close on

Left: Cook's crew collecting ice to take aboard for drinking water, 9th January, 1773.

Inset: True-to-life portrait of Captain James Cook, from a painting by William Hodges.

mid-summer's day in the southern hemisphere) describes this ice and its dangers: *"Steered SE along the edge of the pack till we came to a point round which we haul'd SSW, there appearing Clear Sea in that direction. But after running 4 Leagues on this course, always along the edge of the Ice, we found ourselves surrounded by it, for it extended in all directions, farther than the eye could reach, in one compact body, some Few places except'd where Water was to be seen like Ponds. In other places narrow creeks ran in about a mile* (1½ km) *or less. High mountains of ice were seen within this Field, and many an Island of Ice in the Open Sea: also Whales, Penguins and other Birds. We spent the night standing off under Top-sails, it being so foggy we could not see a ship's length. Betwixt midnight and 7 in the Morn 4 inches* (10 cm) *of Snow fell on the Decks, so that our Rigging and Sails were decorated with Icikles."* A month later, on 17th January 1773, Cook managed to force his way across the Antarctic Circle, (being) "the first and only Ship that ever cross'd this line." But the summer was ending, the ice thickening, and Cook had no option but to sail away from the pack and continue his exploration at a lower latitude.

By the end of the season he had explored the Indian Ocean so thoroughly he had proved that a Great Southern Continent couldn't possibly exist there.

Next summer, after wintering in New Zealand, he carried out a similar "ice-cruise" in the Pacific.

As *Resolution* again approached the Antarctic Circle, the ship was again brought up short by ice. Before long the word "ice" was appearing in almost every line of Cook's Diary. *"THURSDAY 16th DECEMBER: Weather dark, gloomy and very cold; our Sails and Rigging hung with Ice and Icikles . . . SATURDAY 18th: Moderate breezes; thick Foggy weather with Snow and Sleet which froze to the Rigging as it fell, so that everything was cased with Ice . . . TUESDAY 21st: A strong gale attend'd with thick Fogg; our Rigging so loaded with Ice we could scarce get our top-sails down to a double-reef . . . FRIDAY 24th: Wind northerly: a strong gale with thick Sleet and Snow which* froze to the Rigging. Our ropes became like wire, our sails like plates of metal . . . I have never seen so much Ice. The whole World was covered in it."

Any ship – even a 20th century ice-breaker – would have found it difficult to survive in these conditions. For an 18th century square-rigged collier to survive, month after month, was little short of a miracle. For *Resolution* had to be sailed from its exposed deck. In order to set the ship's sails, reef them and 'hand' them, men had to go aloft frequently and in large numbers. In bad weather – and the weather was bad 90% of the time – a seaman's life was at risk each

time he left the deck. Even to touch the rigging was to face frost-burn that seared like flame, and to fight the iron-hard sails aloft meant bloodied hands, minced fingers and nails torn out by the root. *Resolution* survived partly because of its double-wooden hull, and partly because of Cook's exceptional skill as a seaman.

In his second season of exploration Cook sailed for great distances, far closer to the Pole than anyone had ever sailed before. This voyage proved that the Great Southern Continent didn't exist in the Pacific.

In his final season, after putting ashore

Cook's ship Resolution *among the Antarctic ice floes with* Adventure *in the background, a painting by J. Webber.*

briefly in Tierra del Fuego, Cook explored the Atlantic.

The *Resolution* had now been away from England for 2½ years. The crew were eager to get back to their families, and Cook's survey of the Atlantic was nothing like as thorough as his survey of the Indian and Pacific Oceans. This was ironic. For it was here, and here alone, in the southwest extremity of the Atlantic that he might have discovered, not only chain after chain of sub-Antarctic islands, but the continent itself. As it was, *Resolution* was homeward bound, when on Friday 13th January 1775, Cook sighted the only bit of unknown land he had come across since leaving England. His first thought was that he must have stumbled at last on the Great Southern Continent, albeit much reduced in size. Further exploration, however, proved it was an island he had discovered, South Georgia: *"a terrain savage and horroable, the rocks raising their lofty summits till they were lost in clouds, the Vallies buried in everlasting snow . . . Who would have thought* (Cook went on) *that an Island situated at the same latitude as England should, in the*

Romanticised portrait of Captain James Cook, by Nathaniel Dance.

The sort of newly-formed ice through which Resolution *had to sail.*

very Height of Summer, be wholly cover'd many fathoms deep with frozen Snow. The quantity of Ice is incredible. Yet this Island alone could not have produced the ten-thousandth part of the Ice that we had met with in the previous years of our voyage. I THEREFORE BELIEVE THERE MUST IN THE FAR SOUTH BE MORE LAND TO WHICH THIS VAST QUANTITY OF ICE ADHERES." A few days later he repeats this belief. *"I firmly believe there IS a tract of land near the Pole, which is the source of all the Ice spread over this vast Southern Ocean. It is, however, true that such a continent must lie quite within the Polar Circile, where the Sea is so choaked with Ice that the Land is inaccessible."*

A few months later *Resolution* was back in England. The voyage had lasted 1,114 days. The ship had sailed 108,630 kilometres (almost three times around the world). Not one of the crew had died from scurvy.

Many people think that the voyage of the *Resolution* is the greatest voyage ever made – myself, I would place it second only to Magellan's. It was a great voyage partly because it was so long, so difficult and so dangerous; and partly because it added so much to our knowledge of the world.

Before it, every map of the world contained a mythical "Land of Brazil Wood, Elephants and Gold" which occupied almost a third of the globe. After it, Antarctica was reduced to its true nature and proportions, a land "inaccessible and quite within the Polar Circle."

Such was Cook's reputation that no-one questioned his findings. There was a widespread feeling that if he couldn't discover Antarctica then nobody could. It was therefore many years before another major expedition went there. Then, in the 1820s, reports filtered through to Europe that "a Great New Mainland" had been sighted south of Tierra del Fuego.

2 The First Landing

Nobody can say for certain who was first to sight the mainland of Antarctica, nor who was first to set foot on it. However, I believe myself that the first person to sight it was probably the great Russian explorer, Thaddeus von Bellingshausen, and the first person to land on it, a little-known American sealer, John Davis.

In his Diary Cook had described the penguins, whales and seals that he saw in the Southern Ocean. Seals in the early 19th century were particularly valuable; and it wasn't long before the fishermen of New England, on the east coast of America, were heading into the Antarctic to hunt the creatures for whose rich oil and warm fur there was an inexhaustible demand.

These New England sealers have been called "probably the toughest crews who ever put

Leopard seal (Hydrurga Leptonyx): one of the many species of seal which attracted hunters to the Antarctic.

to sea." They followed a brutal trade in treacherous waters, suffering appalling hardships and often working literally up to their waists in blubber and blood. No wonder they were hard! It has been estimated that in 20 years they killed more than 4,000,000 seals; and it wasn't long before the breeding grounds on the rocky South American beaches had been hunted to extinction. This meant that the sealers had to seek their quarry farther afield: first in Tierra del Feugo, then in the South Sandwich and South Orkney Islands, and finally on the coast of Antarctica itself.

In the summer of 1820/21 John Davis of New Haven, Connecticut, arrived in the South Orkney Islands aboard his ship *Cecilia*. He found that the best beaches for sealing were already occupied, and he and his crew were warned off by their rivals "with Guns, Pistols and Swords." Davis wrote: *"We concluded it best to go on a Cruse to find new lands, as the seal is done for here."* He sailed the *Cecilia* south into unknown waters.

On February 1st Davis landed on Low Island, some 80 kilometres from the Antarctic coast. This landfall can be confirmed by his accurate description of the island, and the fact that when the sun put in a brief appearance, Davis managed to fix his position by taking solar observations. During the next week some 1,000 seals

The American explorer Charles Wilkes, and his ship Porpoise.

were clubbed to death on Low Island. Then, in heavy snow, the *Cecilia* again headed south. Next morning Davis's log gives a prosaic description of what must have been a spectacular discovery. *"Wednesday 7th February 1821. Commences with Cloudy Weather and Light Winds a standing for a Large Body of Land in that direction S.E. At 10 a.m. close in with it, out Boat and sent her in Shore to look for Seal, but found none. Stood up a large Bay, the Land high and covered intirely with Snow. I think this land to be a Continent."*

It was indeed a continent on which the crew of the *Cecilia* were the first human beings ever to set foot, their landfall almost certainly being Hughes Bay on the Antarctic Peninsula. And if you ask why so important an event isn't recorded in history books, the answer is partly because the log of the *Cecilia* has only recently been found, and partly because the discoveries of *all* sealers are shrouded in mystery and contention. For to a sealer new lands meant new beaches; new beaches meant new breeding grounds; new breeding grounds meant profitable cargoes. They didn't therefore proclaim their discoveries but kept them to themselves. Nobody was ever sure just where the sealers had been to; and until recently it was believed that the first landings on the mainland were made by three big expeditions which arrived almost simultaneously off Antarctica in the summer of 1839/40.

Of these expeditions, that of the American Charles Wilkes was perhaps the greatest. For in near-foundering ships and with a mutinous crew, Wilkes charted the coast of Antarctica

for more than 3,000 kilometres: a magnificent feat of seamanship. The expedition of the Frenchman Dumont D'Urville was perhaps the most important scientifically. For although he discovered only a small strip of coast (Adélie Land), D'Urville's account of his exploits is one of the most factually detailed and beautifully illustrated works in the literature of exploration. But it was the expedition of the Britisher James Clark Ross, which led to the most spectacular discoveries.

Ross was one of those lucky people, "born with a silver spoon in his mouth", who seem to have everything: wealth, ability and good looks. He went to sea at the age of 12, spent nearly 20 years searching for the elusive North West Passage, and was the first person to reach the North Magnetic Pole. What Ross didn't know about handling ships in the ice wasn't worth knowing. In 1839 he was offered

The French explorer Dumont D'Urville, and his ships Astrolabe *and* Zelée.

command of an expedition whose aim was to study the Earth's magnetic field in the Southern Ocean. For this he was given first class warships, the *Erebus* and *Terror*, specially strengthened for work in the ice. He was also given first class equipment and stores, and hand-picked crews. Indeed it would be hard to imagine a better-found expedition than that which sailed from the Medway in Kent in the autumn of 1839.

Ross had been in the Southern Ocean almost a year when he heard that French and American expeditions in the same area were investigating reports that land had been sighted beyond the Antarctic Circle. He decided that his orders were sufficiently flexible for him to investigate too. In the Arctic Ross had often sought advice from the people who had local knowledge: the Eskimos. Now in the Antarctic he did the same. He listened to the gossip of sealers, who told him that round about longitude 180° a lagoonlike strip of water was believed to exist beyond the pack-ice. Ross decided, with his specially strengthened ships, to try to break through the pack and explore this open water beyond.

As *Erebus* and *Terror* headed into what is now known as the Ross Sea, the feeling of their crew was summed up by the flagship's doctor, Robert McCormick: *"Our future promises to be full of interest, for we may soon make great discoveries in a region of our globe fresh as at creation's dawn."* But on January 2nd, 1841, the ships were brought up short by pack-ice.

It stretched in front of them as far as the eye could see: a field of white, solid at the edge but with occasional leads of open water inside it. The ships sailed back and forth, searching for somewhere to enter; but there seemed to be no gap in the ice. Ross took a chance. He ran full-tilt at the ice. Again and again the bow of the *Erebus* smashed into the edge of the pack-ice. An ordinary ship would have been stove-in; but after about an hour's hard thumping the *Erebus* and *Terror* managed to force their way into some small patches of open water. *"From here,"* wrote Ross, *"we pursued our way though the pack, choosing the clearest 'leads' and forcing the interposing barriers, at times sustaining violent shocks which only ships*

specially strengthened could have endured." By nightfall they had penetrated many kilometres into the ice.

Antarctica, however, was not to yield its secrets easily.

Next day the ice closed up and thickened, and *Erebus* and *Terror* became frozen in. Then the weather worsened; the swell steepened and widened, the wind increased to a full hurricane, the pack split up, and great waves thick with solid blocks of ice came sweeping down on the imprisoned ships. Again and again miniature icebergs weighing many tonnes crashed into the storm-tossed vessels. *Erebus*'s rudder was split, and the sheathing was ripped from the ship's hull. *Terror* lost its rudder completely, and almost sank. Ross thought their last moment had come. But the storm was too violent to last; after twelve hours of terror the wind dropped, and the damaged vessels were able to limp for shelter behind a line of icebergs. As soon as they had made some much-needed repairs, they renewed their progress through the ice, which had been broken-up by the storm. On January 8th they became the first ships in history to break through the pack-ice into the open water beyond. The way to the continent lay open.

Robert McCormick wrote: *"Monday, January 11th. At 2.30 a.m. land was reported from the crow's nest. It appeared at first indistinctly through haze and light cloud . . . but by 9 a.m. the coast was sufficiently well defined for me to get a sketch. It extended from S.E. to S.W., very high and enveloped in snow. The upper part appeared to be a glaciation, relieved at intervals by the apex (summit) of some dark peak. It soon became clear that we had discovered a new land so extensive and attaining such altitude as to justify the appellation (name) of a Great New Southern Continent."*

It was indeed a great new continent which now unfolded in front of Ross's eyes. All day he sailed towards it, marvelling at the grandeur of the mountains, the dazzling white of the snow, the brilliance of the light, and the silence that hung over his advancing ships. Next morning he made a landing.

It was an incongruous ceremony. The officers were in full dress uniform. The boats

Left: the British explorer James Clark Ross. Above: a painting by J. E. Davis of the first sighting of the Ice Shelf by Ross's ships Erebus *and* Terror.

almost capsized in the heavy swell. Penguins "opposed the landing with raucause cries". Eventually, however, the British flag was raised, and Ross took possession of the newly discovered continent. This was the first fully documented landing on Antarctica.

For several weeks *Erebus* and *Terror* followed the coastline south, from a distance of only five or six hundred metres. All previous explorers had seen Antarctica only from a distance, from *outside* the pack-ice. Ross and his crew were the first people to be able to ap-

preciate the continent's splendour at close range, from *inside* the pack. And on 15th January they were greeted by a scene of the utmost grandeur: a great chain of mountains, many of them over 3,000 metres high, stretching south in an unbroken sweep from sea to sky.

Ross's next discovery was even more spectacular. *"January 28th,"* (writes McCormick) *"we were startled to see a stupendous volcanic mountain in a high state of activity. At 10 a.m., upon going on deck, my attention was arrested by what apepared to be a fine snowdrift, driving from the summit of a lofty crater-shaped peak. As we made a nearer approach, however, this apparent snowdrift resolved itself into a dense column of smoke, intermingled with flashes of red flame, emerging from a magnificent volcanic vent, in the very centre of a mountain range encased in eternal ice and snow. This peak, which rises to an altitude of 12,400 feet, (3,780 metres) was named after our ship, Mount Erebus."*

19th century vessel in high seas off the coast of Antarctica.

The following day Ross made another great discovery. To the south-east of Mount Erebus his path was blocked not by a coastline, but by a perpendicular wall of solid ice: a barrier smooth as marble, apparently unending, and three times the height of the ship's mast. *"It presented an extraordinary appearance* (writes Ross) *seeming gradually to increase in height as we got nearer, and proving to be a perpendicular cliff of ice, about 200 feet (60 metres) high, perfectly flat at the top and without any fissures or promontories on its seaward face. What lay beyond it we could not imagine . . . but we knew we might as well try to sail through the cliffs of Dover as penetrate such a mass."* He had discovered one of the eight natural wonders of the world: the ice-barrier which bears his name.

Ross followed the Ice Shelf east for 400 kilometres, searching for somewhere to spend the winter. However, it grew loftier and, if poss-ible, even more forbidding. There was no flaw in its defences, no gap into which his ships could squeeze. Eventually, with fresh ice beginning to form on the sea, Ross was obliged to haul away to the north, and to try once again to force his way through the pack. He had a dangerous passage, at one point nearly being dashed to pieces against a chain of icebergs; but eventually he fought his way clear, and set course for Tasmania.

Not till the autumn of 1843 did *Erebus* and *Terror* return to England, having been away for 4 years and 5 months. This was one of the longest and most successful expeditions in the history of the Royal Navy.

Ross's achievements are, deservedly, well-known. Seas, ice shelves, capes and mountains are named after him. He was a great explorer. But it is worth remembering he was *not* the first man to set foot on the mainland of Antarctica. That honour probably belongs to the little-known American sealer, John Davis.

Icebergs in Erebus and Terror Gulf.

3 The First Winter

The big expeditions of the 1840s and the voyage of John Biscoe in the 1830s indicated that the new-found continent would be difficult to explore and impossible to colonise. So there now began a period when everyone knew Antarctica existed, but no-one wanted to go there.

Towards the end of the 19th century, however, scientists were beginning to realise that the ice-continent might well be "a refrigerated storehouse of knowledge", and that its untrodden wastes might well hold valuable clues to the evolution of our planet. In 1895 the International Geographical Congress declared that "the unveiling of this unknown land is the most important piece of exploration still to be undertaken," and it urged scientific teams to go there. From now on the old-fashioned search for land was replaced by the more modern search for knowledge.

First to respond to this new ideal were the Belgians. In 1894 Adrien de Gerlache, a lieutenant in the Belgian Navy, presented a paper to the Royal Geographical Society of Brussels suggesting that an expedition be sent to the coast of the Antarctic Peninsula. After three years of fund raising, experimenting and training, his dream was realised.

It was a small, well organised team of scientists who sailed from Ostend on 24th August, 1897. Their ship, the *Belgica*, was an ex-sealer, a tough little battering ram of a vessel, lacking beauty or comfort but ideally suited for work in the ice. *Belgica* was sheathed in both greenheart wood and Swedish iron. This ship's stern was one-and-a-half metres thick; and the bows were angled up (like the runners on a sledge) so that it was possible for the ship to ride over the edge of the ice. The ship's doctor, Frederick Cook (not to be confused with Captain James Cook) wrote of her: *"In harbour she*

The Belgian explorer Adrien de Gerlache de Gomery, and his ship Belgica *(opposite).*

looked like a bull-dog amid greyhounds, small, awkward and ungraceful: but she was to prove a craft of extraordinary endurance, withstanding the thumps of rocks and icebergs in a manner perfectly marvellous." The crew was cosmopolitan. The captain, first lieutenant and five seamen were Belgian. The mate and four seamen were Norwegian. The geologist and the meteorologist were Polish. The naturalist was Rumanian, and the doctor American. Among them were men who were to become famous: Henryk Arctowski who pioneered the study of Antarctica's climate. Doctor Frederick Cook who claimed to be first to reach the North Pole, and Roald Amundsen who was undoubtedly first to reach the South Pole.

It was as well they were men of courage and ability. For they were soon to be tested beyond the normal limits of endurance.

The expedition spent two months in Tierra del Fuego studying the Ona and Yaghan Indians; they then carried out a useful survey of the sea-bed between the southern tip of

America and the northern tip of the Antarctic Peninsula. It was January before they entered Hughes Bay, the site, some 80 years earlier of Davis's historic landfall. During the next month the *Belgica* sailed continuously south along the Antarctic coast, making as many as 19 landings, at each of which her crew collected valuable scientific data. Then they made history. Five of them left the *Belgica* and spent almost a week ashore, thus becoming the first men to camp and sleep on the new-found continent. It was a terrifying experience. *"Our first night,"* wrote Doctor Frederick Cook, *"was one of stormy discomfort. A wind came out of the glacier above us, against which we could hardly stand. It took two men to hold up the tent, and the combined efforts of all hands to prevent our effects* (belongings) *being blown over the cliffs only a few yards away. On 1st February we struggled a few yards into the interior, but fog wind and crevasses made frequent halts necessary. The sledges were almost impossible to move, and the difficulty of travelling and the discomfort of camping made life difficult in the extreme . . . After a stay of 7 days, the first camping experience in the history of south polar exploration, we gladly betook ourselves back to the Belgica."*

This was mankind's first indication of how difficult Antarctica was going to be to explore. It had taken de Gerlache and his crew a week to penetrate a single kilometre into the interior; and at least one of them, Amundsen, recognised the foolishness of trying to cross such country by using sledges hauled by men.

Mid-February found the *Belgica* still forcing its way down the Antarctic Peninsula, smashing through pans of ice one-and-a-half metres thick, and elbowing aside floes 60 metres in diameter. De Gerlache has been criticized for continuing south so late in the season, long after the time when most ships in the Antarctic were hurrying home. But he was taking a calculated risk. He knew his ship was well-built, and well-stocked with fuel and food; and he reckoned that his crew would have no dif-

ficulty surviving the winter. He was not therefore too worried when the ice thickened, and they became frozen-in. This was in a position 71°22′S, 84°55′W: about 500 kilometres inside the Antarctic Circle and 1,800 kilometres from the Pole.

Here, on the edge of the known world, the *Belgica* and its crew were held fast, unable to move, like flies trapped in amber.

There was nothing particularly new in the idea of an expedition being frozen-in for the polar winter. Eric the Red had allowed this to happen to him in the 10th century during his exploration of Greenland; and many Arctic explorers, such as Barents, Parry, Franklin and Nordenskjöld, had followed his example. No-one, however, had ever attempted to survive a winter in the Antarctic. And this, as de Gerlache now discovered, was a very much sterner test.

At first their imprisonment was more unpleasant than dangerous. De Gerlache and his companions did their best to make themselves safe and comfortable by surrounding the *Belgica* with a wall of ice blocks, by covering up the companionways, by double-boarding the portholes, and by experimenting with heating and ventilation. Meanwhile snow fell without respite hour after hour, day after day, week after week, month after month. *"If only,"* de Gerlache lamented, *"we could be quit of this infernal humidity. It is impossible to keep anything dry: clothes, equipment and bunks are all the time beaded with moisture and veneered with ice."*

This may not have been dangerous, but it was definitely depressing; and as summer turned to autumn the crew's depression gave way to anxiety – anxiety about the *Belgica*. For by now, to quote her doctor, Frederick Cook, the ship had become *"a football of fate: kicked, pushed, squeezed and driven this way and that at the mercy of the pack . . . March 16th. The ice suddenly cracked all about us, being forced together by the most terrible pressure. Huge hummocks rose up on every side, as the floes were forced one over the other and against the vessel. Wood was gouged out of her hull, and she was thrown onto her side across a floe, where she lay enduring the bat-*

The West coast of the Antarctic Peninsula off which *Belgica was trapped by sea-ice.*

tering of the ice with cracks and groans . . . But at last the pressure eased, and she settled back onto an even keel."

As winter set in the ice became more stable, and it soon became reasonably certain that the *Belgica* would survive. It was a different story with the crew. For as the sun disappeared completely and their world became shrouded in what seemed to be never-ending night, they began to suffer from anaemia, scurvy, paranoia and a host of delusions and disorders. What caused their mental and physical deterioration was a combination of cold, humidity, isolation, wind and, above all, total darkness.

The temperature that winter never rose above zero. The humidity was depressing; out of the *Belgica's* 347 days in the pack-ice it was foggy on 255 days, and snowed on 271 days. The isolation was absolute, the crew being cut off from the rest of the world as effectively as if they had been marooned on another planet. Strong wind was found to be as harmful to human health as cold; and most of the time that winter it blew a near-gale. It was, however, the darkness that affected them most. In early May the sun, like a faintly glowing lump of charcoal, still appeared briefly above the horizon. But on May 17th it disappeared altogether, and it didn't come back for 68 days. To quote the log of the *Belgica*:

"Now the members of the expedition became affected, body and soul, with a terrible languor (lack of energy). *Each man continued to do his duty, but did it painfully. Polar anaemia preyed on them all. In some, the pulse rate rose to 150 per minute, in others it sank to 47. The lack of fresh food made itself felt; by mid-winter de Gerlache, Malaerts and Michotte were showing symptoms of scurvy. One seaman had bouts of hysteria which bereft* (deprived) *him of reason. Another, unable to bear the pressure of the ice, went mad with terror. On June 5th Lieutenant Dance died of heart failure . . . The root cause of all these disasters was the lack of sun."*

This judgement is confirmed by Doctor Cook:–

"During the months of winter darkness the life-giving rays of the sun are withdrawn, leaving the Earth in total blackness. Artificial light relieves this to some extent; but all animal organism is left in a condition similar to that of a planet deprived of sunlight. The skin grows pale, muscles grow weak, and the organs are unable to function with their usual vigour. This effect is most noticeable in the action of the heart which, deprived of its regulating force, becomes now quick, now slow, but never normal. The best substitute for the sun is direct heat from an open fire. I have stripped and placed men whose pulse was almost imperceptible in this sort of heat, and in less than an hour their heart action has returned to normal."

It was due largely to Cook's heat treatment that all but one of the *Belgica's* crew were still alive when, on July 22nd, the sun reappeared, "like a small withered orange," on the rim of the horizon.

When the sun reappeared, hope was reborn. The *Belgica*, it is true, was still held fast in the ice; but as the days lengthened, the crew's energy and will-to-live returned. Sledge parties set out to explore the surrounding pack-ice, and attempts were made to blast the ship free with explosives. The ice, however, couldn't be shifted. Fifty kilograms of explosive did no more than scoop out a shallow depression. This was seen at first as no more than a temporary setback; but as spring gave way to summer and summer to autumn, and the *Belgica* still couldn't move, the crew began to view with terror the prospect of another winter in the ice.

Cook, and de Gerlache thought out a way to save them. The entire crew set to work to cut a canal, two kilometres long, through the pack-ice. The difficulties were enormous. Ice more than a metre thick had to be cut away by hand-saw. New ice formed almost as fast as the old was cut. The pack shifted, temporarily closing their canal. But at last they managed to fight their way through to the open sea. Their ordeal was over. On 28th March 1899 the *Belgica* steamed into Punta Arenas in Chile, having spent 13 months inside the Antarctic Circle during 12 of which the ship had been frozen solid into the pack.

De Gerlache and his crew were both heroes and pathfinders. They were the first expedition members to survive an Antarctic winter. They were also the first to penetrate deep into the Antarctic for the sole purpose of collecting scientific facts. The data they brought back was of great scientific value. But perhaps of even greater value was the tradition they helped to establish: the tradition of people risking their lives to acquire scientific knowledge, and, on their return to civilization, making this knowledge freely available to everyone who was interested throughout the world. Outside his native Belgium, de Gerlache is little known. He was, however, a great explorer.

4 The Race for the Pole

The race between Amundsen and Scott to be the first person in the world to reach the South Pole is *not* typical of the way Antarctica was explored. Most explorers fought Antarctica together. It is because Amundsen and Scott tried to fight one another as well as the Antarctic that their race ended in tragedy.

Roald Amundsen was born in southeast Norway in 1872. When he was fifteen, his parents gave him an unusual Christmas present: the works of Sir John Franklin, the British naval officer who lost his life in the Canadian Arctic while searching for a North West Passage. These stories so thrilled the young Amundsen that he made up his mind to become an explorer.

Many young people dream of being explorers; few have ever worked as hard as Amundsen did to make their dreams come true. In midwinter he slept with his window open, "to toughen myself up". Although he disliked football, he played it "to train my body to endure fatigue". He volunteered for military service, "not because I wanted to fight but to strengthen my physique." At the age of twenty-two, Amundsen was serving aboard an Antarctic whaler, and at the age of twenty-five was de Gerlache's mate in the *Belgica*. A few years later he managed to succeed where his hero Franklin had failed: he became the first person in the world to discover and sail through the North West Passage – the seaway from Atlantic to Pacific *via* the ice-bound north coast of Canada. Amundsen then decided to try to become the first person to set foot on the North Pole. However, just as his expedition was about to sail, he heard that the American explorer Peary had claimed to have reached the North Pole.

Amundsen changed his plans. If he couldn't be first at the North Pole, he would be first at the South! He set course not for the Arctic, but the Antarctic.

Some historians have criticised him for this. They say he knew that the British explorer Scott had just sailed for the Antarctic and hoped to be first to reach the Pole. They say that by also heading for the Pole, Amundsen introduced an element of competition: that he started a race. It seems to me, however, that the lonely places of the world should be open to the explorers of *every* nation, and the idea that the British had some sort of monopoly on them was unjustified.

So in 1910 two expeditions were heading south, Amundsen's and Scott's. But apart from the fact that they were both bound for the Pole, they had little in common.

Amundsen, in his ship the *Fram*, was in charge of a small close-knit team of nineteen men, all competent skiers and dog-handlers. When he reached Antarctica he intended to rely on one form of transport only, dogs; and these dogs were looked after with unprecedented care. As the *Fram* sailed through the tropics, Amundsen even went to the trouble of building a false deck to keep them cool. He had one objective only: to be first at the Pole.

Scott, in his ship the *Terra Nova* was in charge of a very different sort of expedition: a mixed party of sixty-four scientists, naval officers and naval ratings. When he got to Antarctica he intended to experiment with many forms of transport – man-hauled sledges, motor-sledges, dogs and ponies. He had several objectives; for as well as making a dash for the Pole, his orders required him to survey both the coast and the interior, and to carry out an exacting programme of scientific research.

From this you can see that Amundsen's expedition was simple, with all its energies channelled into one objective. Scott's expedition, on the other hand, was complex, and its objectives were diverse and often conflicting. You could almost have predicted the way each expedition would end from the way it started out.

Amundsen sighted the coast of Antarctica early in January, 1911. For several days he ran parallel to the Ross Ice Shelf, searching for

The Norwegian explorer Roald Amundsen, and his ship Fram.

somewhere to land. On January 13th he found what he was looking for: a spot in the Bay of Whales where the ice was stable and not too high. Here he set up his winter quarters, Framheim, about 1,400 kilometres from the Pole. The Norwegians sited their hut three kilometres from the sea in a position which was sheltered and safe. They had just got the building erected, when they had unexpected visitors. The *Terra Nova* came sailing into the Bay of Whales.

The events of the next forty-eight hours disprove the myth that Scott and Amundsen didn't like one another. They were rivals, but they were not enemies. Visits were arranged between ship and shore. The British offered to take home the Norwegian's mail. The Norwegians offered to share their winter quarters with the British, and to give them half their dogs. *"Scott was a splendid man,"* wrote Amundsen, *"and nobody could hold a higher admiration than myself for his courage."* The British, however, decided to set up their own base in McMurdo Sound, at the opposite end of the Ice Shelf.

As soon as Framheim was built, the Norwegians started establishing food depots along the route by which they intended next spring to travel to the Pole. During February and March they established three such depots, the most southerly more than 300 kilometres from Framheim; these they stocked with 4½ tonnes of food. Then winter closed in. *"For a couple of days,"* wrote Amundsen, *"the sun rested like a bright red ball on the horizon, surrounded by a sea of flame; then it vanished behind the pressure ridge to the north. We were not to see it again for four months."*

The Norwegians spent a spartan but trouble-free winter at Framheim. Much of the time they rested. Indeed Amundsen was so anxious that his men should not overtax themselves that he ordered them not to take meteorological readings by night, in case their sleep was disturbed. This was in contrast to Scott's winter at McMurdo Sound, where the British carried out a programme of very de-

Right: Scott's hut in McMurdo Sound, painted by Edward Wilson, 14th May 1911.

manding scientific research. Another big difference between the expeditions was that life in the Norwegians' hut was free and easy, with the explorers all living together and all on Christian-name terms with their leader; whereas the British hut was divided into a wardroom for the officers and a mess-deck for the ratings, with naval discipline very much the order of the day.

The return of the sun on 24th August found the Norwegians and their dogs *"in good health and high spirits, fairly bursting with energy and eager to be on our way."* By 19th October the weather had improved sufficiently for the assault party of five men and fifty-two dogs to set out for the Pole.

The first part of their journey lay over the Ice Shelf. They made good progress; for their dogs were fresh and their sledges light. They carried little food; partly because they planned to use the provisions they had stored the previous autumn, and partly because they planned, in due course, to kill and eat some of their dogs. Most of the time they allowed themselves to be towed on skis behind their sledges. Only when they came to difficult ground did someone ski on ahead to blaze the trail. They averaged 40 kilometres a day, and soon arrived at the first of their food depots.

The fact is that thanks to his excellent planning, Amundsen's task was proving easy. Indeed, he and his men had so much time to spare that on the next stage of their trek across the Ice Shelf they stopped every few kilometres to build snow beacons. These were almost two metres high and were marked with flags. Buried in each beacon was a waterproof paper, giving the course to steer in order to get to the next beacon. These proved a great help on their journey back.

On November 6th the Norwegians passed the last of their food depots. They were in virgin country now, and could see ahead of them the great semi-circle of unknown mountains, today called the Queen Maud Range, which form the boundary between the Ice Shelf and the central plateau. *"So far,"* writes

One of Amundsen's cairns in the Queen Maud Range, still standing after 70 years.

Amundsen, *"our journey has been a pure pleasure trip, with both weather and surface as favourable as one could wish. Everything has gone swimmingly. On November 16th we approached the spot where the coastline intersected our route. To start with this presented little difficulty, the ice simply swelling up in a succession of ridges, some 300 feet (90 metres) high, like waves, approaching a shore. We established a depot here, then pressed on, carrying food for 60 days. The terrain ahead, which we had to ascend looked formidable: a chain of steep, glacier-clad mountains, some 10,000 feet (3,050 metres) in height, with a further chain of almost 15,000 feet (4,600 metres) seen dimly to the southeast. Next day we began the ascent."*

The weeks that followed were the most arduous of the journey. For the mountains proved difficult to climb, with a succession of ice-falls, glaciers and innocent-looking snow-slopes which were found on closer inspection to be criss-crossed by a network of hidden crevasses. The names on Amundsen's map conjure up the hazards: 'Hells' Gate, Satan's Glacier, The Devil's Ballroom'. Once, less than a metre from his tent, Amundsen uncovered a deep and apparently bottomless hole: *"So that no more than a couple of feet (60 cm) from our front-door, we had a handy way down to the cellar!"* Several times men and dogs found themselves dangling over ice-blue crevasses anything up to 300 metres deep. Several times too they had to sledge over snow "that trembled and quivered like blancmange." But at last they struggled through to the rim of the central plateau, and saw ahead of them the great white and featureless plain that guards the approaches to the Pole. Here they killed half their dogs.

It was a sad occasion. Amundsen was not as sensitive to the fate of his animals as Scott. He was, nonetheless, reluctant to kill them. *"It was hard,"* he writes. *"But it had to be. We had agreed to shrink from nothing to achieve our goal. I am not a nervous man, but at the sound of the first shot I found myself trembling. Shot soon followed shot in quick succession, echoing uncannily over the great white plain. Each time a trusted servant lost his life."*

The weather, as if in retribution, now worsened; and for a fortnight the Norwegians could only creep forward through a succession of blizzards. December 3rd, however, dawned fine and clear, and from then on progress was rapid. Indeed crossing the plateau was so easy that if Amundsen's men hadn't known they were drawing ever nearer to the Pole, they would have been almost bored. In every direction, as far as the eye could see, lay the same flat featureless expanse of white. The world seemed to consist of nothing but length and breadth. Day after day there was no sound but for the scuffing of skis, the creaking of sledges, the scratching of the dogs' feet and the occasional crack of a whip. In the early afternoon of December 14th, Helmer Hanssen, who was driving the lead-sledge, shouted to Amundsen: "Will you go on ahead?"

"What for?"

"The dogs run better with someone in front of them."

By this trick the Norwegians made sure that their leader was first at the Pole.

When they reckoned they were in exactly the right place, the Norwegian flag was unfurled, and photographs were taken showing each of the five explorers grasping the flagpole. It was an historic moment: the conquest of what is one of the loneliest and most inaccessible point on Earth. And it is proof of Amundsen's greatness as an explorer that so difficult a goal was so easily achieved.

The Norwegians spent three days at the Pole, sledging over a wide area to be certain they had indeed set foot on it, erecting cairns and tents and leaving messages for Scott. *"He will be here sooner or later,"* Amundsen said to Hanssen. *"I hope for his sake it will be sooner."* Then, on December 17th, they started the return journey to Framheim.

Knowing the tragic events that overtook Scott on *his* return, one might have expected that the Norwegians would have been in some difficulty if not danger. Not a bit of it. *"We travelled,"* wrote Amundsen, *"chiefly by night with the sun and the wind behind us. The going was splendid. We were in high spirits and bowled along at a cracking pace. We had no difficulty in finding the way, for our snow beacons stood out clearly. And we had no difficulty keeping to our daily target of 17½ miles* (28 kilometres), *usually covering this distance in less than 5 hours. The dogs looked sleek and well-cared for. The men had prodigious appetites and actually put on weight . . . We had so much food we often left behind caches of biscuit and pemmican. We fed chocolate to the dogs."* They arrived back in Framheim, in perfect health on January 25th – the very day which Amundsen had earmarked as ideal for their return. A week later his expedition, in the warmth and comfort of the *Fram*, was on its way home.

Amundsen had triumphed.

But Scott, some 800 kilometres to the south, was in trouble. On the very day that the *Fram* sailed for home, the entry in the British explorer's diary hints at the tragedy to come: *"Friday, February 2nd. Three out of five of us injured. We shall be lucky if we get through. We are desperately hungry, our bags are wet, and we ought to have more sleep."*

How, one wonders, can things have gone so well for one expedition and so badly for the other?

*   *   *

Robert Falcon Scott was born in Devonshire in southwest England in 1868. Unlike Amundsen, he never wanted to be an explorer; he wanted to be, and indeed became, a naval officer. It was while he was serving aboard the *Active* in the West Indies that he met Sir Clements Markham, then the president of the Royal Geographical Society. Markham, in those days, was the driving force behind British polar exploration; and in 1900 he offered Scott command of the *Discovery*, a vessel which he had fitted out for research work in the Antarctic. Scott, with considerable misgivings, accepted. So you might say he became an explorer by accident. This helps to explain Scott's shortcomings. He was *not*, like Amundsen, experienced in polar conditions; he was *not* a skier, and he was *not* good at handling sledge-dogs. He was an able and conscientious naval officer, who suddenly found himself commanding not ships but sledges.

In spite of his lack of experience Scott's first expedition (1901–4) was successful. He spent three years in the Antarctic, carried out useful survey work, and brought back an enormous amount of scientific data. Indeed the information obtained by this one expedition takes up more space on the library shelves than the entire 24 volumes of the *Encyclopaedia Britannica!*

In 1909 Scott decided to head south again, but this time in command of a larger and more ambitious expedition: an expedition which intended to survey the coast and the interior, to collect scientific data, *and* to attempt to reach the Pole. These conflicting aims spelt trouble, and were the basic reason for Scott's failure. Another reason for his failure was his indecision over how to travel. He took with him motor-sledges (which broke down), ponies (which were basically unsuitable), and dogs (which he didn't trust). In the end he decided to travel by man-hauled sledge. This was a mistake. For as Amundsen points out: *"Conditions on the Antarctic ice-cap are ideal for sledging with dogs. It seemed to me a fundamental error for the British not to use them. Perhaps the dog didn't understand his master – or was it that the master didn't understand his dog?"* With this last comment, the shrewd Amundsen hits the nail on the head; although in fairness to Scott it should be said that as well as not understanding his dogs, he disliked using them on humanitarian grounds. Markham explains this very clearly. *"With regard to dogs there are two ways to treat them; either you bring them back all safe and well, or you get the greatest amount of work possible out of them and then use them as food. Scott had an unconquerable aversion to using them this second way."* To confirm this, Scott himself wrote: *"No journey made with dogs can approach the sublimity of a party of men who succeed by their own unaided efforts. Surely in this* (latter) *case, the conquest is more nobly and splendidly won."* These sentiments do great credit to Scott as a man; to Scott as an explorer they were to be his epitaph.

The British explorer Robert Scott, and his ship Terra Nova.

The right and the wrong way to travel in Antarctica: sledges hauled by dogs, and sledges hauled by men.

Scott arrived in Antarctica at much the same time as Amundsen, and set up his winter quarters in much the same area (the Ross Ice Shelf). But whereas the Norwegians then concentrated all their efforts on using their dogs to establish food-depots, the British attempted many different jobs in many different ways. Scott sent a food-carrying party to the south, a geological survey party to the west, and an exploring party to the east; he also sent a team aboard the *Terra Nova* to the Ross Ice Shelf, and left another team in McMurdo Sound to improve their winter quarters. Some of the explorers travelled by man-hauled sledge, some by dog-hauled sledge, some by pony and some by motor-transport. This diversity was fatal; and as autumn gave way to winter, it became obvious that the achievements of the British did not equal their efforts. Probably no men ever worked harder or more selflessly. But their motor-sledges proved unworkable, their dogs proved intractable, and their ponies died. They managed to establish only one small food depot less than 150 kilometres from their base. And, what was worse, Scott became so disillusioned by the repeated failure

of his transport, that he decided to rely on the one motive-force which he felt would never let him down. He decided to try and reach the Pole by means of sledges hauled by men.

The winter of 1911 passed pleasantly for the British. *"We are quite overwhelmed,"* wrote Scott, *"with the comfort of our quarters."* The British explorers did, however, spend a great deal of time and effort on scientific research. Three of them, for example, very nearly froze to death while studying the winter hatching of emperor penguin chicks. This work was highly commendable; but it was not the ideal preparation for an assault on the Pole.

With the coming of spring, Scott and his companions were soon on their way to the Pole. They set out on 23rd October, 1911 – just four days later than Amundsen – a motley team of tractors, ponies, dogs and men. They were soon in trouble. Their tractors seized up. Their ponies couldn't stand the cold and had to be shot. The men could hardly move the sledges over the heavy snow. *"We are wet through,"* wrote Scott's companion Bowers. *"Our tents are wet, our bags are wet, our food is wet; everything on round and about us is wet ... It is all we can do to keep the sledges moving forward for short spells of perhaps 100 yards (90 metres). The starting is worse than the*

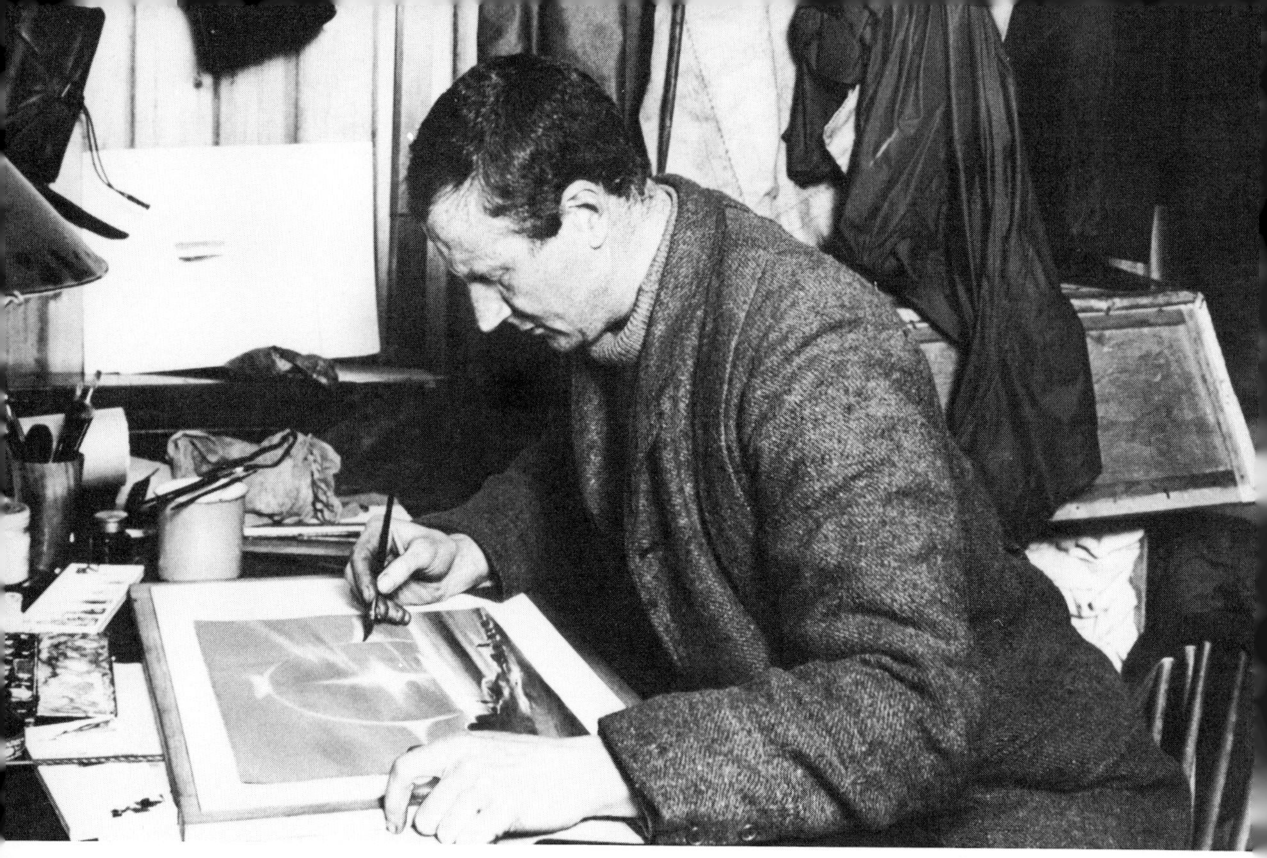

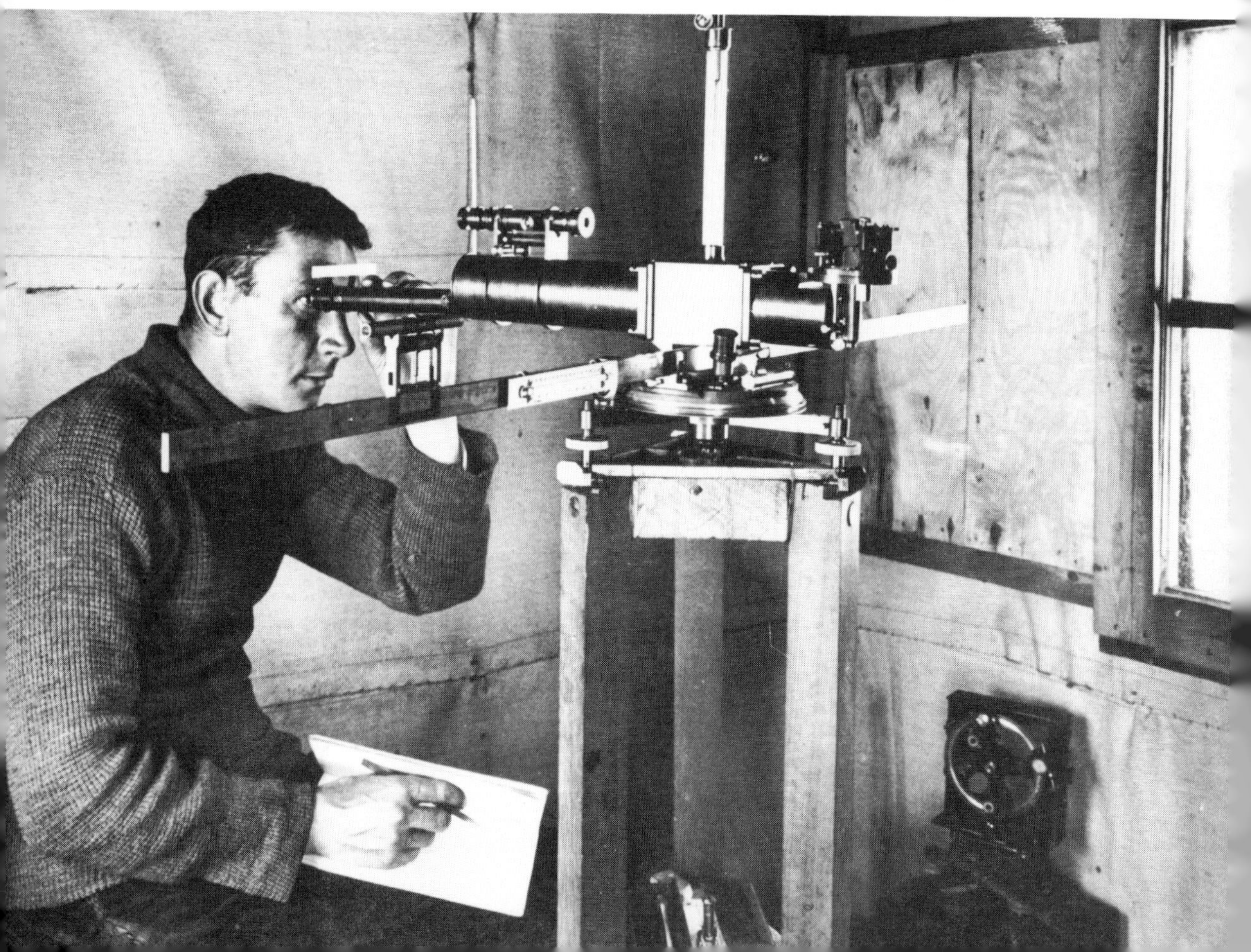

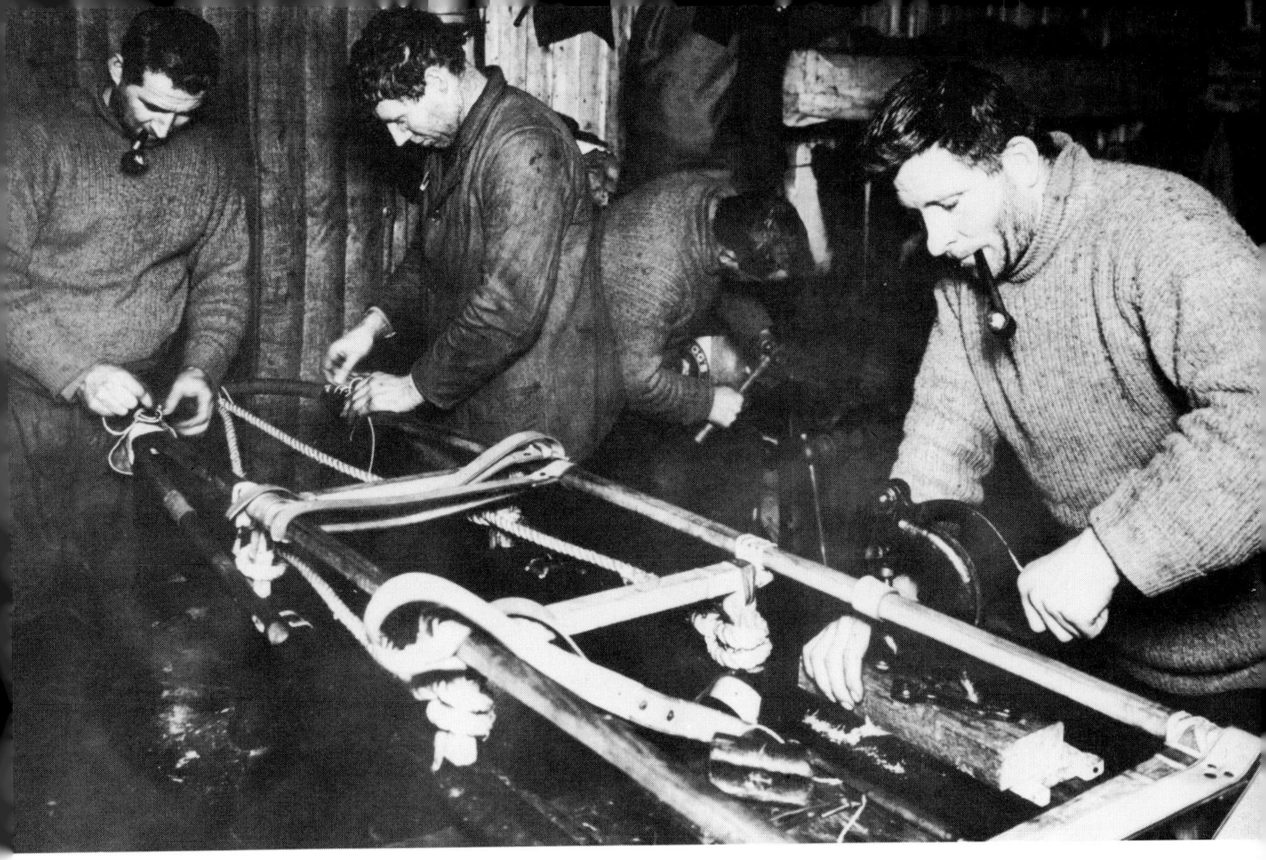

Members of Scott's expedition at work. Upper left:
The artist Edward Wilson finishing a sketch. Bottom
left: Operating the magnetometer. Above: Assemb-
ling sledges. Below right: Measuring the water
level. Below: At the sewing machine.

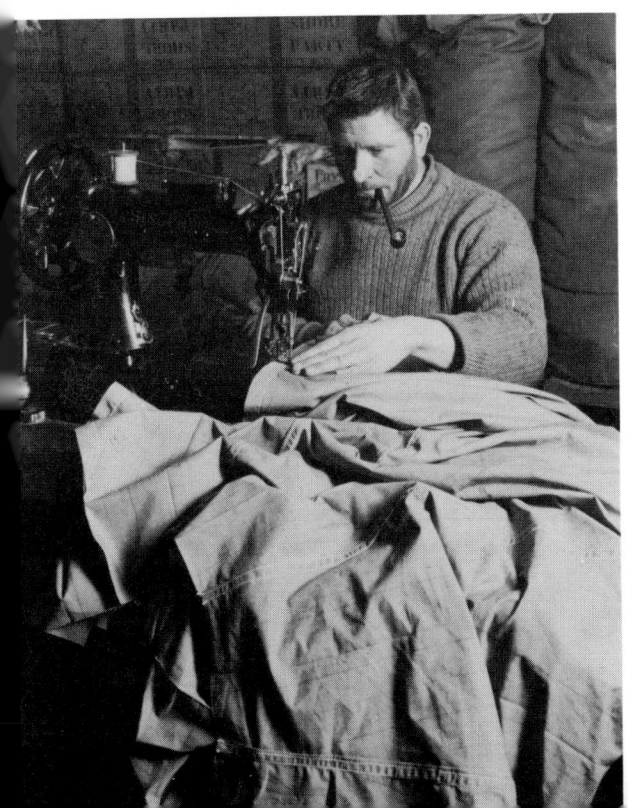

pulling: it requires from ten to fifteen desperate jerks on the harness to move it all." What a contrast to the Norwegians' easy 40 kilometres a day with their sledges hauled by dogs!

On 4th January, 1912, some 270 kilometres from the Pole, the last of the support parties turned back, and Scott and his four companions – Bowers, Evans, Oates and Wilson – set off on foot on their journey of no return. They were now in the same latitude as Amundsen; but Amundsen had already reached his objective and was on his way back.

What happened next has an air of tragic inevitability. It may seem a harsh judgement, but the truth is that Scott's poor planning and his lack of experience as an explorer now caught up with him, and he and his companions paid for his mistakes with their lives. Scott made a lot of little mistakes. His food depot wasn't far enough to the south – if it had been 20 kilometres closer to the Pole he would have been able to reach it on his return journey. On his final dash to the Pole he took four men with him instead of three. His food was insufficient and ill-balanced. On his return journey he travelled by day instead of by night. None of these mistakes would, by themselves, have mattered. But together, combined with the vital fact that his sledges were hauled by men and not by dogs, they tipped the scale between survival and disaster.

On their way to the Pole Scott and his companions, manhauling their sledges, made slow and physically exhausting progress. *"I've never known such pulling,"* Scott wrote in his Diary. *"We covered 6 miles (9½ kilometres) today, but at fearful cost to ourselves."* At last, on January 16th, 1912, they reached the Pole, only to find flags and a cairn. Amundsen had beaten them to it. *"The Norwegians have forestalled us,"* wrote Scott. *"It is a terrible disappointment . . . it will be a wearisome return."* The return, however, was to prove a great deal worse than "wearisome".

With winter approaching, Scott and his companions couldn't afford to rest; nor with their food running short, could they afford to eat the big meals that their physical labour demanded. They could only struggle on, becoming progressively weaker. It wasn't long before they

began to break down physically. First to go was Evans, suffering from frostbite and scurvy. He went on pulling, as best he could, right to the end; but on 17th February he collapsed in his traces. That night he went into a coma, and in the small hours of the morning, he died. Next to go was Oates. His frostbitten feet turned black with gangrene. Every step he took was agony. He never complained, but he knew that he was holding the others back. Early one morning he crawled out of the tent, saying: "I am just going outside, and may be some time." He limped away into the storm, and was never seen again. "It was," wrote Scott, "the act of a brave man." His sacrifice, however, was of no avail. On March 21st Scott, Bowers and Wilson pitched their tent for the last time. Crippled and starving, they knew that if the blizzard didn't subside, they would die. How they spent their last few days we know from Scott's Diary.

One might have expected Scott's Diary to be depressing. It isn't. It is inspiring. And it is this Diary, I think, which transforms the British expedition from a chronicle of failure to a story of courage and determination in the face of the most terrible conditions. Scott was not a great explorer. But he was a good, and in some ways a great, man. This is evident from the last pages of his Diary, written shortly before his death.

"We are pegging out in a very comfortless spot. In a desperate state, feet frozen etc., no fuel and a long way from food; but it would do your heart good to be in our tent, and to hear our songs and cheerful conversation as to what we will do when we get to Hut Point . . . (Later) We are very near the end, but have not and will not lose our good cheer." In a last message to his mother he wrote: *"Take comfort in that I die at peace with the world and myself – not afraid."*

Scott, Bowers and Wilson died on about 31st March, 1912. Bowers and Wilson died in their sleeping bags – perhaps in their sleep – Scott with his bag open.

The British expedition had ended in tragedy, you might say in failure. But one thing never failed: the courage of the men. This courage has earned Scott and his companions an honourable place in history.

5 "Endurance"

There has never been a greater feat of seamanship than Shackleton's open-boat voyage from Elephant Island to South Georgia after the loss of his ship the *Endurance*.

Ernest Shackleton was a member of Scott's first Antarctic expedition of 1901–4, and a few years later came close to being the first man to reach the South Pole when he sledged to within less than 150 kilometres of it. He was a larger-than-life figure. The establishment didn't approve of him because he was outspoken and unconventional; but those who sailed with him respected and loved him. He was a great leader.

His ship the *Endurance* was part of an ambitious expedition which in 1914 attempted to cross Antarctica. The plan was that one ship, the *Aurora*, should land men on the Pacific Ocean side of the continent, and these men would set up food depots along the route to the Pole. Meanwhile at the same time another ship, the *Endurance*, would land men on the opposite side of the continent; and these men would cross Antarctica *via* the Pole; picking up the food left by the *Aurora* on the final stage of their journey.

The *Aurora* had a difficult time. She was swept by blizzards into heavy ice, and pounded very nearly to destruction. It took the ship two years to struggle back from Antarctica to New Zealand. The men who were left behind on the Ross Ice Shelf suffered terribly from cold, exhaustion and hunger, and several died.

But the ordeal of the *Aurora* was nothing like so dramatic as the ordeal of the *Endurance*.

The *Endurance* arrived in the Weddell Sea late in 1914. It was a bad year for ice. While the ship was still 160 kilometres from the coast she became ensnared, trapped fast without a hope of escape, by the thickening ice-floes. Shackleton tried frantically to cut and batter his way clear. *"But the task,"* he wrote, *"was beyond our powers, and I realised we would have to spend the winter in the inhospitable arms of the pack."*

For month after month the *Endurance* drifted this way and that at the mercy of wind and current. To start with she was not in serious danger; but with the approach of spring the ice caused them anxiety. Like some monstrous flower whose sap was rising, the ice began to move. The floes first split with a crack like a whip, and then piled up one on top of another. Worst of all were the pressure ridges: great walls of ice advancing like slow-moving waves over the surface of the pack. In mid-October the *Endurance* was trapped between two converging ridges. She was flung onto her side and squeezed until she broke up.

Shackleton's crew describe her last hours. *"Closer and closer the pressure wave approaches,"* writes the expedition's photographer Frank Hurley. *"Now it is within a few yards* (metres) *of the vessel. We are helpless, and can only look impotently on. The line of pressure assaults the ship, and she is heaved to the crest of the ridge like a toy. Immense blocks of ice are forced under her counter and wrench away her stern post. The carpenter announces that the water is gaining rapidly on the pumps. All hands are ordered to stand by to abandon ship. The pumps work faster and faster; someone is singing a shanty to their beat, as the dogs are passed down a canvas chute, followed by rations, sledges and equipment. The ship is doomed."* Shackleton was the last to leave. *"It was a sickening sensation,"* he tells us, *"to feel the deck breaking up under one's feet, the great beams bending then snapping with a noise like gunfire. I looked down the skylight, and saw the engines drop sideways as the stays and bed-plates gave way. I cannot describe the impression of relentless destruction. The floes, with the force of millions of tons* (tonnes) *of moving ice behind them, were simply annihilating the ship."* Late that evening, as her crew watched from the comparative safety of the ice, the *Endurance* gave literally her last flicker of life. *"You could hear the ship being crushed. As the ice ground into her, you felt as if your own ribs were cracking. Suddenly, inside her, a light went on for a moment and then went out. It seemed like the end of the world."*

The *Endurance* had gone, and with her Shackleton's dream of an Antarctic crossing. As he and his twenty-seven men stood huddled together on an ice-floe, hundreds of kilometres from land, and with no hope of outside help, Shackleton had one objective only: survival.

He salvaged as much as he could from the *Endurance* before she disappeared beneath the ice; then he tried to head for Paulet Island, some 640 kilometres to the north. The going wasn't just difficult, it was impossible. In some places the floes were thick, rafted together to form ridges four to six metres in height; in other places they were so thin that the sledges fell through them into the ice-cold water beneath. Sometimes the ice was so hard they couldn't chip it away even with picks; other times it was so soft that dogs and men found themselves floundering waist-deep in slush. At the end of an exhausting week, they had travelled less than 15 kilometres to the north, and the current had drifted them more than 8 kilometres to the southeast. Shackleton realised that his men would die of exhaustion long before they reached Paulet Island. He therefore decided to camp on the most solid floe he could find, wait for the ice to melt, and then take to the ship's boats which had been salvaged from the *Endurance*. A few days after Christmas 1915, he established a camp called 'Patience'. Here, cold, wet, short of food and in conditions as miserable as any on Earth, he and his ship's company settled down to wait.

Throughout the late summer, as the ice on which they were camped melted, conditions in Patience became increasingly difficult. Heavy snowfalls kept the men confined to their tents for nineteen days out of twenty. *"We all became very weak,"* writes Shackleton. *"As fuel was so scarce, we had to resort to melting the ice for drinking-water by holding it in tins against our bodies . . . Our meals were practically all seal meat, with a single biscuit midday . . . On April 2nd we shot the last of our dogs."* That they survived at all was remarkable. That they survived with cheerfulness

is evidence of Shackleton's qualities as a leader.

"You felt," one of his crew tells us, *"that so long as the Boss was in charge everything was going to be all right. He was undefeatable."* And Shackleton was not only respected; he was loved. He never claimed any privileges for himself because of his rank – "if he had half a pipe of tobacco, he'd share it." To his men he always appeared confident that somehow and against all the odds they were going to survive. Only those who shared a tent with him knew the long agonising hours that he spent in coming to his decisions, the endless lists that he made to cope with every foreseeable emergency, and the doubts and fears that night after night prevented him from sleeping.

By the end of the first week of April, the great icefield in which the *Endurance* had been crushed had thinned down and drifted to within sight of the South Shetland Islands. It had now broken up into a number of individual floes, on one of which was Camp 'Patience'. A heavy swell made the floes heave and quiver; it jostled them together, breaking them into ever smaller fragments. Cracks began to open up without warning in even the most solid-looking surface, so that men who were one moment asleep in their tents would next moment be tumbled into ice-cold water. Three times Shackleton saved members of his crew from drowning.

By 9th April Patience was impossible to live in. The camp had become a morass of slush which would neither float a boat nor support a man. As they drifted into a patch of open water, Shackleton gave the order to take to the ship's boats, which had been salvaged from the *Endurance*. There now began a three-day voyage of appalling hazard: a voyage in which Shackleton and his men were many times within a hairsbreadth of death.

The South Shetland Islands, bleak and uninhabited but offering a temporary haven, lay about 100 kilometres to the north-west. To reach them the three little overcrowded open boats had to cross seas that were lashed by constant gale-force winds, swept by great

Ernest Shackleton and his ship Endurance *trapped in the pack ice.*

Left: Endurance *crushed to death by the ice.*
Above: Camp Patience, the new quarters for the crew after the loss of their ship.

waves more than fifteen metres from trough to crest, and strewn with great blocks of ice. *"Our deeply-laden boats,"* wrote Shackleton, *"made heavy weather. They shipped spray which, freezing as it fell, coated men and gear with ice. But at least we were on the move!"* One of his party, Frank Worsley, gives an even more graphic description. *"A howling gale was blowing, and a terrific sea running. One moment we were on the crest of a tremendous swell – you could see right away to the horizon, nothing but sea and ice and sky – then you'd drop into the hollow and see a great roller coming towards you filled with blocks of ice . . . The temperature fell to 36° (−20°C) of frost. It was so cold that our overalls crackled, and ice and frost fell off us as we rowed. When the moon came out, we saw that our beards were white with frost, moustaches were knobbed with ice, and each man's breath formed clouds of vapour, showing white against the darkness of his face."* Packs of killer whales, dangerous as sharks, kept pace with the boats: waiting for them to capsize.

The boats nearly capsized and nearly foun-dered many times during that terrible cross-ing; but at last, after three nightmare days, they managed to struggle into a bleak but sheltered cove on the coast of Elephant Island. *"Many of us,"* writes Worsley, *"were light-headed by now. Some reeled about, laughing uproar-iously. Others sat on the shingle, and, like harmless lunatics, let it run through their fingers. It was the first land we had set foot on for 485 days."*

The men's most urgent needs were food and warmth. And they were lucky. Within a couple of hours of landing, they found and killed an elephant seal. The great creature's flesh gave them meat for the most nourishing stew they had had for months, and its blubber fuel for the warmest fire. They were, for the moment, out of danger.

The prospect of death, however, hadn't vanished; it had only receded. Elephant Island was uninhabited, unbelievably bleak, and far from the usual track of sealers and whalers; it was a place no-one would think of looking for them. They could, Shackleton realised, survive on the island for a short spell; but not in-definitely. Many of his men were too weak to attempt another voyage in the open boats. Shackleton therefore had no option but to try and get help. The nearest land to the west was

Above: The open boats setting out for the nearest land – Elephant Island – after their camp became untenable.

Right: The James Caird *sets off from Elephant Island for South Georgia and opposite: Saved!*

Cape Horn; that was only 650 kilometres away; but Shackleton knew that he hadn't a hope of sailing there against the constant gale-force winds. The nearest land to the east was the island of South Georgia, where Shackleton knew there was a whaling station which was manned all the year round. But South Georgia was 1,700 kilometres away. To get there he would have to navigate with pinpoint accuracy, not for days but for weeks, through the most tempestuous and dangerous seas on Earth.

Most people would have thought it impossible. Shackleton set about strengthening one of his boats, the tiny *James Caird*. On 23rd April, together with five of his crew, he set off on one of the most hazardous voyages ever attempted.

Before they were out of the bay, the *James Caird* very nearly capsized, and two of her crew were flung into the sea and almost drowned. Before they were out of sight of land, the boat had twice very nearly been crushed like an eggshell between colliding blocks of ice.

Shackleton divided his men into two watches, four hours on and four off. During his duty watch one man took the tiller, one was in charge of the sail and one baled. Those off duty could, in theory, sleep, though in practice they were usually too cold, wet and cramped.

No-one has described their voyage better than Shackleton himself.

"The sub-Antarctic Ocean lived up to its evil reputation. Deep were the valleys and high the hills. So small was our boat that its sail would flap idly in the calm between the crests

of the waves. Then we would climb the next slope and catch the full fury of the gale, as the whiteness of breaking water surged all about us. Always there were gales. Many times we were in dire peril . . . On the fourth day a severe southwesterly gale forced us to heave to. I would have liked to run before the wind, but the sea was too high and the James Caird was in danger of broaching to and swamping. We put out a sea anchor to keep our head up; but even then the crests of the waves would curl right over us and we shipped a great deal of water. A thousand times it seemed as though the boat must be engulfed; but somehow she lived . . . By daylight on the sixth day the James Caird had lost her resilience. The weight of ice in her and on her was having its effect, and she was becoming more like a log than a boat. It was a situation which called for desperate action. We broke away the spare oars, which were encased in ice and frozen to the side of the boat, and threw them overboard; two of our four sleeping bags also went over the side. This reduction of weight relieved the boat to some extent, and vigorous

chipping did more. We had to be careful not to put axe or knife through the frozen canvas, but gradually we got rid of a great deal of ice, and the James Caird lifted to the waves as though she lived again . . . On the tenth night Worsley could not straighten his body after a spell at the tiller. He was thoroughly cramped, and we had to massage him before he could unbend enough to get into a sleeping bag. A hard northwesterly gale came up in the late afternoon . . . At midnight I was at the tiller and suddenly noticed a line of what looked like clear sky to the southwest. I called to the others that the weather was clearing, then a moment later realised that what I had seen was not a rift in the clouds but the white crest of an enormous wave. During 26 years' experience of the ocean in all its moods I had not encountered a wave so gigantic. It was a mighty upheaval of the ocean, a thing apart from the big white-capped seas that had been our enemies for days. I shouted 'For God's sake, hold on!' There came a moment of suspense that seemed drawn out into hours. Then the foam of the breaking sea surged white

South Georgia: the reindeer were successfully introduced by Norwegians in 1911.

around us. We felt our boat lifted and flung forward like a cork in breaking surf. We were in a seething chaos of water; but somehow the boat lived through it, half-full of water, sagging deadweight, and shuddering under the blow. We baled with the energy of men fighting for life . . . On the thirteenth day thirst took possession of us. Lack of water is the most severe privation that men can be condemned to endure, and we found that the salt water in our clothing and the salt spray that continually lashed our faces made our thirst grow into a burning pain . . . Things were bad for us those last few days, but the end was coming. At about 12.30 p.m. on May 8th we caught sight, through a rift in the clouds, of the black cliffs of South Georgia."

It is hard to know which to admire most: the men's endurance, Shackleton's leadership, or Worsley's navigation.

Their troubles, however, were not over. For no sooner had they sighted land than the wind

increased to "one of the worst hurricanes any of us had ever known"; and the *James Caird* was in danger of being swept to destruction against the ice-coated cliffs of the island. Desperately they fought their way away from the land; until late that evening wind and sea subsided, and they drifted, battered and exhausted, onto a little beach, where, as if in answer to their prayers, a stream of fresh water cascaded from glacier to sea. After 16 days' sailing through the most dangerous seas on Earth, it seemed like a miracle.

One last difficulty had to be overcome. The whaling station lay on the opposite side of the island. Two of Shackleton's crew were by this time desperately weak; they had been driven close to insanity by their ordeal, and were in no condition to continue the voyage. In any case, Shackleton realised it would be highly dangerous to try to sail round South Georgia's cliff-bound coast. The quickest way to the whaling station was by land: directly across the island. The island, at the point where they had landed, was no more than 80 kilometres wide. But these 80 kilometres consisted of a precipitous range of 2,000 metre mountains.

The fact that the mountains were coated from base to summit in ice and had never been crossed, would have daunted most people. But after a couple of days' rest, Shackleton and his two fittest companions set out for the whaling station.

They had virtually no equipment; no tent or sleeping bag, only some 15 metres of rope, and the carpenter's adze to use as an improvised ice-axe. They knew they had to keep moving, or they would freeze to death. They climbed on and on: all through the day, and all through the following night. They knew if they stopped not only would *they* die, but their shipmates whom they had left behind would die also. At one point they coiled-up their rope, sat on it and slid into the darkness down a 70° snow slope, descending 750 metres in three minutes! At another point they were so exhausted and bemused that they thought a fourth man was with them on the rope, guiding them, helping them. They climbed non-stop for 24 hours, until at last, almost too wonderful

The cross marking Shackleton's grave in South Georgia.

to be true, they saw beneath them the whaling station at Husvik.

After more than twenty months' imprisonment in the polar ice, with his ship long since reported as lost with all hands, Shackleton had made contact with the outside world.

The finale of Shackleton's expedition reads like a fairy tale come true. Within 48 hours of his arrival in Husvik, a whalecatcher had rescued his men from the opposite side of the island. Soon Shackleton himself was aboard a Chilean ice-breaker and on his way to Elephant Island. He was only just in time.

"Are you all well?" he shouted anxiously as he came within hailing distance of his marooned ship's company.

"All safe," came the reply. "All well."

Shackleton's face lit up, and a great burden seemed to fall from his shoulders. Never, on any of his previous expeditions, had he lost a single man serving under him. Many times in the last two years it must have seemed to him that he was going to lose the entire crew of the *Endurance*. But once again, after one of the most hazardous expeditions in polar history, he managed to bring every one of his ship's company safely home.

6 The Air Base at the Bottom of the World

The American explorer Richard Byrd.

In the summer of 1911/12 Amundsen and Scott had struggled through to the South Pole, the latter at the cost of his life. It was 44 years before anyone else reached the Pole, a time-lag which underlines the difficulties of exploring Antarctica. Not until 1956 did another group of people, seven Americans, stand triumphant at the bottom of the world. And the Americans got there by a very different method from Amundsen and Scott. They came by air.

The man who did most to pioneer the use of aircraft in Antarctica was the American Richard Byrd. Byrd was born in Winchester, Virginia in 1888. He had two loves, exploring and flying, and managed to combine them in a way that was unique. *"It became my ambition,"* he wrote, a few years after qualifying as a Navy pilot, *"to make my career in aviation: not in the sense of routine flying but in the pioneering sense. At the time I was learning to fly, the airplane was becoming a tool which mankind could fit to its hand. My ambition was to test this tool to the utmost, through a series of long-range flights."* In the early 1920's Byrd made an aerial survey of North Greenland, and in 1926 became the first person in the world to fly over the North Pole. When the explorer Amundsen asked him where he was going next, he replied, "to the South Pole." This was the seed from which, 30 years later, grew the U.S. air base at the bottom of the world.

Byrd spent a long time preparing for his flight to the South Pole – he called it "the hardest three years work of my life." Even so, he was very nearly defeated by the most hazardous conditions for flying in the world. He arrived off the Ross Ice Shelf on Christmas Day 1928, with two ships, three aircraft, hundreds of men, thousands of tonnes of equipment and tens of thousands of litres of aviation fuel. He knew that it wouldn't be easy to fly to the Pole. He therefore planned first to establish a base, then to reconnoitre and map a route, then to spend a winter at his base, and finally to establish a half-way airstrip at which his plane could refuel on its way to the Pole.

Byrd chose the position of his base with the greatest care; for he needed ice which was not only sheltered, but was also level enough and stable enough to act as a landing strip. He found what he was looking for a little to the east

The Queen Maud Range as photographed from Byrd's aircraft.

of the Bay of Whales; and soon a mini-village, which he called 'Little America', was springing up along the edge of the Shelf. There were three main buildings, built of orange prefabricated sections and placed some 100 metres apart so that an accidental fire in one would not endanger the others. There were also about a dozen smaller buildings, three aircraft hangers hollowed out of the snow, a cluster of 20-metre radio masts, and a store for their thousands of litres of fuel. *"Little America,"* wrote Byrd, *"is a beautiful and eerie location. Out beyond the shacks, the wireless masts and the spectral shapes of the planes, it is as quiet as a tomb. Nothing stirs. The silence is so deep one feels one can reach out and take hold of it."*

A couple of weeks after their arrival came an historic moment. The first plane ever to take off from Antarctica, a Fairchild monoplane, lifted clear of the ice. An hour later it landed safely. This first flight gave Byrd a foretaste of both the hazards and the rewards of flying in the Antarctic. It was so cold that before take-off the Fairchild's engine and engine-oil had to be heated by an acetylene torch held under fireproof covering. Icicles froze solid onto the plane's control surfaces. When it taxied out to take-off eight men had to hold down its wings to prevent it being blown over. Once in the air its compass proved useless because of the proximity of the South Magnetic Pole, and its pilot found that the glare from the ice was blinding, and that distances were almost impossible to judge. This was a distinct handicap when it came to landing! However, on the credit side, the crew had a magnificent panoramic view, and in less than an hour were able to photograph and roughly survey more than 2,500 square kilometres of virgin ice.

Throughout the latter part of the summer Byrd probed at the approaches to the Pole. Because of the weather, flying was possible only about one day in six; but when the planes were able to get airborne they achieved fantastic results, discovering range after range of mountains and mapping in hours a greater area than had previously been mapped in decades. It was dangerous work. Every flight called for a combination of care, skill and luck. Accidents were inevitable. On one occasion their Fokker monoplane which had been lashed down for the night began, in the rising wind, to break free from the ropes which tethered it. The men who rushed into the blizzard to try and secure it, found the plane banging up and down and going through all the motions of flying; its propellor was whirling round so fast that it couldn't be seen, and its air speed indicator was reading 140 km/h. They couldn't hold it down. A violent gust of wind, which registered 240 km/h, carried away the last of the ropes. The plane burst free. It soared high into the air, was blown backward for over a kilometre, and smashed against the side of a mountain. The men who managed next day to struggle across to it, found it lying on the ice like the carcase of a great bird, its tail section shattered and its fuselage ripped open. It never flew again.

Soon after this episode Byrd and his men settled down for the winter in Little America. *"We burrowed deeper and deeper,"* he wrote.

"The planes were dragged into deep pits and covered with tarpaulins, the tunnels were roofed over, and the buildings became enveloped in snow. As blizzards pounded the surface, we were snug below. Time didn't drag: for we had plenty to do."

Most of the time that winter they spent preparing for their coming flight to the Pole. Every eventuality was catered for, every detail worked out. For example what they took with them in the plane was calculated down to the last roll of film they would be able to carry in their cameras.

It was several months before the horizon at mid-day was again streaked with light. Then, on August 16th, the men who climbed the radio-masts were treated to a fantastic sight. In the north the orb of the returning sun, magnified by refraction, was flinging up great shafts of red and gold from below the horizon; while in the south the disc of the moon, like a segment of green cheese, hung motionless in a purple sky. But although the sun had returned, the cold remained. It was a couple of months before test-flights and dog-teams were again heading south.

Byrd's plan was to establish his half-way airstrip at the foot of the Queen Maud Range. On

The Queen Maud Range, painted by Edward Wilson.

this first part of his flight he would be supported by dog-teams, so that if his plane was forced down rescuers were likely to be close at hand. Once their half-way airstrip had been stocked with food and fuel, Byrd planned, at the first opportunity, to take off from there for the Pole. This would be the difficult part. For his plane, a Ford trimotor monoplane, couldn't climb above 3,400 metres. Many peaks in the Queen Maud Range rose to 3,800 and even 4,000 metres. He would therefore have to cross the range *via* a glacial pass, which was no easy task for a plane flying in turbulent conditions close to its maximum height.

It was late November before the airstrip was ready; and several times, on this "easy" part of his flight, Byrd came close to disaster. The plane's fuel pump sprang a leak, and had to be plugged with chewing gum. There were engine failures and emergency landings. On several occasions their plane was caught in a "white-out" (or blizzard), which pilots described as "like flying in a bowl of whirling milk." But at last all was ready. November 28th dawned fine and clear. "Go now," the meteorologist said to Byrd. "You'll never have a better chance." An hour later they were airborne for the Pole.

As soon as they left their half-way airstrip, they were faced with the Queen Maud Moun-

tains, drawn up like a line of silver-armoured cavalry across their path. They headed up the Liv Glacier. Flying was difficult. *"The stream of air pouring down the glacier,"* wrote Byrd, *"tossed the airplane about like a cork. The wings shuddered as they dipped this way and that. After awhile the roughness became so violent that we were forced to the left-hand side of the valley. This brought us over a fearfully crevassed slope which led up to Mount Nansen, and here the down-surging currents damped our rate of climb . . . We swung over to the right-hand side . . . Here the glacier floor rose in a series of icefalls and terraces, some of them well above the altitude of the plane. These glacial waterfalls were the most beautiful I have ever seen. Beautiful yes, but with what finality they would deal with us if we crashed into them at 100 miles per hour (60 km/h)!"* Soon they were approaching the moment of truth, the "hump" at the head of the glacier where it joined the polar plateau. They poured the last drop of fuel into their tanks and jettisoned the empty cans; every kilogram of weight lost was a metre of height gained. Their altimeter was now reading 3,000 metres; but the controls were becoming sluggish, the plane was wallowing this way and that, and Byrd could see to his dismay that they were not gaining height. He was in a dilemma. If he jettisoned fuel, they would never get to the Pole; if he jettisoned food, a forced landing would lead to death from starvation. His crew helped him to make a decision; they dragged a 90 kilogram food container to the trapdoor. Byrd nodded. The container spun down, to burst in a soundless explosion on the glacier below; and the plane, as though in gratitude, resumed its climb. But how slowly and hesitantly! Another food container was jettisoned. This did the trick. The plane, with a few metres to spare, scraped over the "hump"; and its crew saw stretching ahead of them the vast and featureless expanse of the central plateau, their pathway to the Pole.

The rest of the flight was an anti-climax. They crossed the plateau without incident, taking sun shots every few minutes to confirm their position. At 1.14 a.m. all calculations agreed they were at the Pole. They didn't land,

A crevasse cave photographed during Byrd's expedition.

but circled the spot taking photographs and dropping American, British and Norwegian flags. *"The Pole,"* wrote Byrd, *"lies in the centre of a limitless plain. And that is all there is to say about it. It is the getting there that counts."*

Later that same morning their plane returned to Little America. The journey which had taken Amundsen and Scott four months had taken Byrd less than sixteen hours.

This historic flight was a turning point. Before it Antarctica had been explored and mapped almost entirely by dog-teams and sledges; after it, it was explored and mapped almost entirely by aircraft. Byrd had added a new dimension to Polar exploration.

It was, however, one thing to fly *over* the Pole, and another to land on it and build a base. This wasn't to happen for another 27 years.

The idea of establishing a base at the Pole which was built, manned and supplied entirely from the air came about as a result of the International Geophysical Year in 1957. The purpose of the IGY was to promote a free exchange of scientific information between the nations. With this in mind it was decided to establish in and around Antarctica 55 obser-

Above: Entrance to the Amundsen-Scott station at the South Pole, covered by a geodesic dome.

Left: Living quarters inside the dome.

vation posts which would be manned by the scientists of 12 countries. The Russians agreed to set up four posts, including one at the Pole of Inaccessibility. The Americans agreed to set up six posts including one at the Geographical Pole. This project was given the code name "Operation Deepfreeze".

"Deepfreeze" was entrusted to the U.S. Navy. A preliminary reconnaissance was made in 1954 by their ice-breaker *Atka*; and as a result of the *Atka's* report it was decided to re-open the base at Little America and to open a new base at McMurdo Sound. The main American fleet, commanded by Admiral Dufek, arrived off the Ice Shelf in the spring of 1955. And what a fleet it was – nine ships, nineteen aircraft, 3,000 men, 10,000 tonnes of

supplies and more than 4,000,000 litres of fuel! Never before or since has so vast a task-force challenged the solitudes of the Antarctic.

The base at Little America was re-opened fairly easily; but the base at McMurdo Sound was another story. The Americans advanced on McMurdo Sound by both land and sea. A sledging party approached the Sound *via* the top of the Ice Shelf, and cargo ships and ice-breakers approached it *via* the Ross Sea. Both ran into difficulties: crevasses in the case of the former, sea-ice in the case of the latter. The ships had a particularly tough time. For a huge iceberg more than 32 kilometres long had grounded across the mouth of the Sound, blocking the currents which usually sweep the ice out to sea each summer. Because of this the ships and their vital equipment found themselves blocked by a solid sheet of ice while they were still 60 kilometres from land. An attempt was made to unload the equipment and drag it ashore by tractor; but this was called off after a tractor plunged through the ice and its driver was drowned. Dufek called on his most modern icebreaker, the 8,600 tonne *Glacier*, which, with great difficulty, carved out a narrow channel to within 8 kilometres of the shore. The channel, however, was littered with sharp ever-shifting blocks of ice, and was a death-trap for ordinary vessels. The supplies had to be laboriously transferred from cargo ships to icebreakers, carried as close as possible to the land, then unloaded and dragged ashore by tractor. It was many months before the buildings were erected, and the landing-area levelled and flagged.

The American base was close to Scott's original winter quarters at Hut Point. It was a strange sensation for those who visited Scott's hut, to look in through the windows and see the rooms unchanged after more than 40 years. A leg of ham (perfectly preserved in the refrigerated air and still edible) was lying on the table, together with sweets, home-brewed beer (still drinkable), a coffee-pot and photographs of King Edward VII and Queen Alexandra; while overhead flew Neptunes and Skytrains of the U.S. Navy.

The Neptunes and Skytrains arrived in mid-

Three great explorers of the Antarctic: left to right, George Dufek, Vivian Fuchs and Edmund Hillary, photographed at the South Pole.

summer after a hair-raising flight from New Zealand. Hair-raising because it is 2,800 kilometres from New Zealand to McMurdo Sound, and the range of the U.S. aircraft was under 2,700 kilometres. In other words unless they had a following wind, they would run out of fuel and crash before they could reach the Antarctic airstrip. Several times the planes took-off; and several times they were forced back by unfavourable weather. But at last four of them got through safely. Soon these four aircraft were taking-off on a succession of hazardous flights, mapping large areas of the Antarctic and reconnoitring the route to the Pole. The key question was: "could a plane land at the Pole?" Some people said the snow would be too soft, some said it would be too rough. There was only one way to find out.

On 31st October, 1956 a Skytrain with a crew of seven including Admiral Dufek, took-off on a historic flight, its objective to be the first aircraft to land at the Pole. The flight was certainly eventful. On its way to the Pole the plane developed an oil leak; over the Pole it had difficulty locking down its undercarriage; and when at last it was ready to land, there was nothing by which the pilot could judge dis-

Aircraft are now often used for scientific work in the Antarctic. Above: An American Globemaster on the sea ice near Mount Erebus. Left: An American UH-1N helicopter, on the Beardmore Glacier.

tance, and he had to come in with the sun at his back, so that the plane's shadow gave him something on which to focus. The trouble was that with the sun at his back he found himself landing not into-wind but down-wind. The touch-down was rough but safe, the plane with the wind behind it leapfrogging on and on over the hard-packed snow. But at last it came to rest, and the seven Americans emerged – the first men since Scott and his companions to set foot on the Pole. *"It was like stepping into a new world,"* Dufek tells us. *"We stood in the*

centre of a sea of snow and ice that extended beyond our vision... . The cold struck me in the face as though I had walked into a heavy door." Within minutes their skin was white with frost-bite. They didn't stay long. They hoisted the American flag, took snow samples and observations, then climbed back into the Skytrain. Take-off was terrifying. For in the few minutes since they landed, the plane's skis had become frozen onto the ice. It needed 15 jet-assisted take-off rockets to blast them into the air.

It had now been proved that a plane could land on the very bottom of the world, and during the next couple of months flights to the Pole became almost commonplace. First an eight-man advance-party, together with dog teams and survival gear, was landed on the plateau. As soon as this party had fixed the Pole's exact position, radar and radio technicians were parachuted down to prepare for an air drop. Soon four-engined planes were droning overhead to deliver food, fuel, pre-fabricated buildings, timber, equipment and snow-tractors. More Navy construction workers were flown in, until "the Pole resembled nothing more than an animated anthill."

The American plan was for 18 men to winter at the Pole. Half of the men would be scientists and half of them servicemen. The base that was being built had therefore to house a great deal of scientific equipment, *and* be warm enough and comfortable enough for men to survive the lowest temperatures on Earth. When finally completed, the building resembled a huge rabbit-warren: more than a dozen compartments connected by a network of roofed-in tunnels. There were sleeping quarters, an eating-area-cum-kitchen, and a recreation room. There were compartments for the meteorologists, the scientists and the radio technicians. There were washing facilities and lavatories – this one compartment alone was larger than the whole of Scott's base at Hut Point. There was a radar tower, an observatory and a powerhouse. There were also internal telephones, hot showers, a light

A Twin-Otter of the British Antarctic Survey on Alexandra Island.

above every bed, linoleum on the floors and film shows three times a week.

This magnificent base was completed on schedule. Then, at the approach of winter, the construction workers were flown out, and the 18 scientists and servicemen settled down to try and survive a night which they knew would be four months long: four months without a glimmer of daylight, and the temperature dropping to −60°C.

They survived, although all of them suffered eye disorders and loss of weight. Their leader, Dr. Paul Siple, describes their principal enemy: cold. *"Just going from one building to another was a serious business; for the temperature in our snow tunnels was −60° (−33°C). At −60° men often find themselves spitting blood, for the capillaries of the bronchial tubes break down. So each time we left a compartment to eat, wash, work or sleep we had to wear face masks and dress up to the teeth."* It says much for the American's hardiness, and for the excellence of their Polar base, that they not only survived but managed to carry out a continuous programme of scientific research.

This research work contributed to the suc-

cess of the International Geophysical Year. And the success of the IGY contributed in turn to the signing of the Antarctic Treaty.

This important treaty guarantees that Antarctica will be used for peaceful and not for military purposes, and that no national claim to territory on the continent shall be recognised. It also guarantees that the resources of the Antarctic will not be exploited haphazardly, but will be conserved sensibly for the benefit of all. It is very much to be hoped that when this treaty comes up for renewal in 1990, it will be accepted as permanent and binding by all the nations of the world. If this happens, then the dream of almost all those who have been to the Antarctic will be realised; and in the words of Byrd's memorial-plaque in McMurdo Sound, *"Antarctica, in its symbolic robe of white, will shine forth as a continent of peace, as nations working together there in the cause of science set an example of international co-operation."*

This is a dream worth caring about and working towards. For Antarctica is not some far-off place that doesn't concern us, but a unique part of our natural world – the heritage of every man, woman and child on Earth.

At work in the Amundsen-Scott South Pole Station:
Above: The Meteorological Office.
Below: The radio operators.

Index

Suggestions for Further Reading

Acknowledgements

Adams, R and Lockley, R. *Voyage Through Antarctica,* 1982

Amundsen, Roald. The South Pole (trans. A.G. Chater), 1912

Byrd, R.E. *Little America,* New York 1931

Cameron, I. *Antarctica: the last continent,* 1974

Christie, E.W.H. *The Antarctic Problem,* 1951

Cook, Dr. F.A. *Through the First Antarctic Night,* 1905

Cook, James. *The Voyage of the Resolution and Adventure* (ed. J.C. Beaglehole), 1961

Dufek, G. *Operation Deepfreeze,* New York 1958

Fuchs, V. and Hillary, E. *The Crossing of Antarctica* 1958

Hosking, E. *Birds of the Antarctic,* 1982

King, H.G.R. *The Antarctic,* 1969

Kirwan, L.P. *The White Road,* 1959

Ross, J.C. *A Voyage of Discovery and Research in the Southern and Antarctic Oceans,* 1847

Scott, R.F. *The Voyage of the Discovery,* 1905
Journals: Scott's Last Expedition, (ed. L. Huxley) 1913

Shackleton, Ernest. *South,* 1919

Stonehouse, B. *Animals of the Antarctic,* 1972

Illustrations which appear in this book are from the following sources: Robert Harding Picture Library – Wally Herbert: Cover and page 36. Dr. Charles Swithinbank's collection: Endpapers, pages 16, 23, 32, 54, 56, 58, 59. National Maritime Museum: Title page and pages 14, 15, 18 (top). British Antarctic Survey, Cambridge: pages 9, 17, 26, 48, 49, 55. Scott Polar Research Institute, Cambridge: pages 18 (bottom), 24, 37, 43, 47, 50, 53 and Back Cover. Norsk-Sjoefarts Museum, Oslo: page 30 (bottom). Baron de Gerlache de Gomery: page 25.

All other illustrations are drawn from the Royal Geographical Society's library and archives. Those appearing in pages 6, 10, 12, 14, 19, 21, 22, 27 and 31 were specially photographed by Robert Glen.

We are grateful for permission to reproduce the map on page 7 redrawn from Ian Cameron, *The Last Continent,* Rainbird Publishing Group Ltd and Robert Harding Picture Library.

Sincere thanks are due to the Baron de Gerlache de Gomery, to Mrs Ann Shirley, to Dr. Charles Swithinbank and Miss Ann Todd of the British Antarctic Survey and to Mr. Harry King and Mr. Clive Holland of the Scott Polar Research Institute. Their advice and helpfulness has proved invaluable.

LONGMAN GROUP LIMITED
Longman House
Burnt Mill, Harlow, Essex CM20 2JE, England
and Associated Companies throughout the World

This book was co-ordinated by Michael Nyman and produced by Pamino Publications, 94 Jermyn Street, London SW1.

Text © Donald Payne 1984

This edition © Pamino Publications 1984

First published 1984
ISBN 0 582 39287 X

Cameron, Ian, *1924 –*

Exploring Antarctica.——(Royal Geographical Society exploring series)
1. Antarctic Regions——Discovery and exploration——Juvenile literature
I. Title II. Series
919.8'904 G863

ISBN 0–582–39287–X

Designed by Tim McPhee
Production services by Book Production Consultants, Cambridge

Printed in Italy by Vincenzo Bona in association with Keats European.